T0209284

STATEMENT
of Faith

What Every Person in Jesus Christ Should Believe

JAMES E. MALONEY, PH.D.

WESTBOW
PRESS®
A DIVISION OF THOMAS NELSON
& ZONDERVAN

WestBow Press books may be ordered through booksellers or by contacting:

WestBow Press
A Division of Thomas Nelson & Zondervan
1663 Liberty Drive
Bloomington, IN 47403
www.westbowpress.com
1 (866) 928-1240

ISBN: 978-1-9736-5553-4 (sc)
ISBN: 978-1-9736-5554-1 (e)

Library of Congress Control Number: 2019902492

Print information available on the last page.

WestBow Press rev. date: 3/8/2019

Contents

What I Believe

If you've ever visited a Christian ministry's Website, most likely you've come across the Statement of Faith, a list of tenets that the organization holds to be true. For the most part, Protestant ministries' statements of faith are similar, highlighting several fundamental truths they all hold in common. Most of these statements are derived from the various Christian creeds throughout the centuries, many of which are recognized by the Catholic church as well as Protestant denominations.

The first of these was the Apostles' Creed (somewhere around 120-150AD), which affirms a Trinitarian God (one Being manifested in three distinct Persons); and that Jesus Christ is Lord, God's only Son, begotten of the Virgin Mary, conceived of the Holy Spirit. It states He was tortured, crucified, died a physical death, was buried, descended into the realm of the dead, and was raised to life again three days later, after which He ascended to heaven and is currently seated at the right hand of God the Father. It further maintains Jesus will return to earth to judge the living and the dead, and ends by confessing belief in the Holy Spirit, the communion of saints (the spiritual union of all members of the Christian church, alive or dead), the forgiveness of sins, the resurrection of the dead, and eternal life. It also speaks of the holy catholic (which means "universal") Church. Even though it is considered a Catholic document, most Protestants adhere to these nearly universal Christian beliefs as well.

However, the Apostles' Creed neglected issuing a statement of faith concerning the divinity of Jesus Christ and the Holy Spirit, though most theological scholars agree it is implicit in the wording. But when the Arianism controversy arose—claiming that Jesus was not preexistent as of the same eternal Substance as the Father (termed "consubstantial") but was later created by the Father and subsequently declared to be God—the Nicene Creed was put forth (first in 325AD, revised in 381AD) to state unequivocally that Jesus Christ and the Holy Spirit are divinely consubstantial with the Father. It is probably the most widely accepted statement of faith in all Christendom.

After the Niceno-Constantinopolitan Creed, the Chalcedonian Creed (451AD) was put forth. This statement is discussed in greater detail in my book *Aletheia Eleutheroo* for interested parties. For the most part this statement is also accepted by the majority of Christian denominations, excepting some Orthodoxy denominations and a larger number of Christian primitivists (Restorationists.)

So even from the early days of the Christian Church, there have been many statements of faith that the preponderance of Christians to this day give credence to. It's important to know *what* we believe and *why* we believe it.

In the last several years, I have been alarmed by a number of "new" theologies (most of them are not actually new, they're just repackaged from doctrines presented over the centuries) that have come to the forefront of charismatic Christian groups, most often springing up from "special revelation"—here I define that as "extra-scriptural"—the proponents of these beliefs claimed to have received. Oftentimes, they're not completely errant or heretical—just a little *off*. And I don't believe, in the vast majority of these cases, the proponents are malicious in their intent to bring these doctrines to the Body of Christ. While we all have to be aware of "wolves in sheep's clothing," most of these proponents are well-meaning. They're not *evil*, they're just somewhat misled, or are not adept at giving a complete definition for what they're trying to say. They'll throw out one-liners without bothering to give a full account of what that one-liner actually means, so it can bring confusion.

Here's a pithy statement: "Half-truths and misquotes are the tools of the enemy." I don't remember who said that originally, it might have been me. *grin*

Sometimes these doctrines stem from partial interpretation of a portion of scripture flawed by faulty hermeneutics, which again is discussed at length in *Aletheia Eleutheroo*. They're ninety percent correct, but it's just taken to an extreme that makes the other ten percent "goofy." We then find umbrella terms for these teachings that often just end up muddying the waters further, so to speak.

For example, I believe in the doctrine of grace, but when taken to an extreme, we get hypergrace. What is the difference between grace and hypergrace?

The doctrine of grace teaches that we have a legal standing in God wherein we are declared righteous (that means, "in right standing") through faith in the atoning work of His Son, Jesus. This is a gift of His grace toward us—it is an unmerited and unearned gift on His part that we have to receive through faith in God the Son. When we accept His

3

JAMES E. MALONEY, PH.D.

grace gift, we are called the "righteousness of God in Him [Christ Jesus]." (2 Corinthians 5:21)

Hypergrace is simply grace taken to the extreme. The most excessive teachings of hypergrace can lead to a sinful lifestyle, because "we have God's grace," so it doesn't really matter what we do. One's actions become virtually irrelevant since the spirit is living in a state of grace. The Bible distinctly teaches against living a lifestyle of sin after becoming a child of God. (Read Romans 6.)

Just because we are living in a state of God's grace does not mean we can live any old way we want. Our actions must line up to the standards in God's Word, and we must renounce a lifestyle of sinning. Does that mean we'll never fall short? No. But it does mean that our heart attitude toward sin must be the same as God's—He hates it, and so must we. Yes, the Lord hates iniquity and sin. (Psalm 5:4-5, 11:5; Proverbs 6:16-19, 8:13; Zechariah 8:17)

But the good news is, if we sin but are repentant, we have a faithful High Priest, Jesus Christ, who is just in forgiving our sins when we confess them and in cleansing us of all unrighteousness. (Hebrews 4:14-15; 1 John 1:9)

The problem is, when someone like myself outlines what I disagree with concerning hypergrace—which, again, is mostly correct until taken to the extreme—it makes it seem like I'm pooh-poohing the doctrine of grace as a whole. I run the risk of being called "anti-grace," which is most definitely untrue. The same goes for dominion theology—I attest to most of the dominion teaching out there; but when we take it to an extreme, we get ultradominionism.

There are many things about ultradominionism I disagree with—the erroneous teaching that we don't have to die a physical death, or that every nation will come to the saving knowledge of Christ before the Second Coming are two examples—but that doesn't mean I throw out *all* concepts of dominion living. I believe Death is the final enemy to be overcome upon Christ's return (1 Corinthians 15:26), and then every knee shall bow and every tongue confess Christ's supreme authority. (Isaiah 45:23; Romans 14:11; Revelation 5:13)

I'm often lumped in with ministers who espouse a particular doctrine, because I've ministered with them in the past, and nay-sayers will unfairly think I believe every jot and tittle of what these ministers have said behind the pulpit. These nay-sayers will often contact me to debate the issues they have with the particular doctrine, and I'm usually like, "Actually I agree with you as much as with them, so what's the problem here?" If I only ministered with people who believed what I believe 100% of the time, I'd have no public ministry!

Many Christians are often all-or-nothing concerning certain doctrines that are not necessarily part of the core theology of Christ. Like, a lot of European Christians consume alcoholic beverages in moderation, a glass of wine with dinner or something similar; most Christians in the West are mortified by this. I think the majority of Christians the world over would agree getting slurring drunk after work is not appropriate behavior for a disciple of Christ, and if a random person off the street can't distinguish between you as a Christian and everyone else at the pub because you're as excessive as they are—that could be a problem. But I've witnessed some majorly heated arguments break out, when in reality, a glass of white wine with your chicken shouldn't have been that big an issue to begin with.

And while there's certainly a doctrine in the Bible about letting your moderation be known to all men (Philippians 4:5), and if we partake of a so-called freedom, it should not be at the expense of someone's else conscience (Romans 14; Galatians 5:13; 1 Corinthians 8:9), that same Bible also teaches love is not touchy (1 Corinthians 13.) To me, that means, pick your battles and don't sweat the small stuff. Don't drink wine around a Nazarene any more than you would eat pork chops around an observant Jew, because the wine or the chops shouldn't be that big of a deal to you in the first place.

I can find a lot of stuff I believe about Baptist theology, but I'm by no means a Baptist minister. I'm not entirely anti-Calvinistic, but I'm certainly not a hyper-Calvinist either. Some of it's right, some of it's off. God *is* sovereign (1 Chronicles 29:11-12; Psalms 135:6; Colossians 1:17); He doesn't predestinate people to go to hell. (Acts 17:30; Romans 8:29-30; 2 Peter 3:8-10)

It is a true statement that Jesus is the Savior of the world. (John 3:17, 4:42; 1 John 4:14) But where much of hyper-Calvinist thought goes wrong is that it is equally true each person must *accept* Jesus as their personal Savior and come into communion with Him. It is conditional, not absolute and automatic.

(I am aware that Calvin himself did not hold this view—and many Calvinists today do not, either, but some hyper-Calvinists do.)

This also means I reject the teaching of Christian universalism, which states that eventually all souls will be reconciled to God (everyone will get saved.) Tragically, they will not.

And certainly, the Bible does not teach that people have a "chance" to accept Christ after their physical death on the earth. (Mark 8:36; Hebrews 9:27)

Some of the traditional Pentecostal beliefs are excessive in my thinking (I have no problem with women wearing trousers, and for all our sakes, everyone, *please* wear deodorant), but that's not to say *all* Pentecostalism is wrong.

I say all this to point out I'm pretty moderate, middle of the road, concerning most of the "extraneous" beliefs certain groups of Christians have over others.

Because I've been in full-time ministry for over four decades and have taught for more than twenty years in Bible colleges, and I have a bunch of alphabet soup after my name concerning theological studies, I often receive e-mails from people asking me "what I believe" about such-and-such (insert a "new" doctrine here or some Christian living question.) The fact of the matter is I don't believe God's called me to be a watchdog for whatever current doctrine is being put forth at the time. I can usually find a middle ground approach to just about anything that's being stated—I minister with Catholics, Baptists, Oneness, even Messianic Rabbis, and most of the time, I get along just fine with them all.

I most certainly do not have all the answers, nor do I claim to be an authority in every area concerning Christian theology. I know a lot, mind you, so this isn't false humility, and I think I'm right most of the time *smile*; but I don't feel it's really my place to attack or defend any particular theological assessment unless it is just clearly antichrist or stupidly unbiblical. I'm pretty vocal concerning things like New Age occult, Universalism, or whatever.

My theology hasn't substantially changed in forty-something years. I still teach the same sermons in my sixties that I taught in my twenties. But again, while I still believe 90% of what I believed in the 1970s exactly the same today, there's 10% that has grown in understanding over the years and will continue to grow till the day I die or meet Jesus in the air. And at that time, all of my questions will be completely answered.

The major problem I see with any slightly wonky theological statement is it usually departs from basic Christian orthodoxy to some varying degree—some tenet of belief that millions of Christians have held for 2,000 years. What alarms me about a lot of these modern teachings is their seeming disregard for what has widely been held as truth for almost two millennia. Just because something is old, doesn't mean it's not still true in the 21st Century as it was in the 16th.

And of course, this isn't a blanket statement. When we read what Christians believed in the Dark Ages, we sometimes have to shake our heads and just go, "Wow..." Or like the Middle Ages and even into the Puritan movement—I don't mind going on record that burning a "witch" at the stake is not the prime example of God's love for all mankind!

But concerning the core beliefs of what it means to call oneself a Christian, most of it still applies the same today as it did in the First Century Church. We would all be wise to balance whatever "new" thing we're hearing with how it holds up to what the majority of historical Christendom has had to say concerning the topic. The adage is true: "There's nothing new under the sun." It's all been said before, just perhaps in a different way.

So that's why this small book was written. Partially to answer most of the questions I receive that ask, "What do you believe about..." And partially to combine quite a bit, but not exhaustively, of what mainstream Christianity has believed since 90 years after Christ ascended, all in a handy-dandy little theology book you can fit in your purse or Bible cover.

I'm not here to convince anyone who disagrees with my beliefs, nor to bash someone over the head who believes something differently than I do. Without the Spirit's conviction that this theology is correct, nothing I can say will change your mind. Try arguing with a Oneness person about the Trinity—see where that gets you! However, I do pray that as you read this, you are open to the Spirit's gentle nudging; and if at the end of this book, you can say, "I agree with 90% of this, I'll meditate on the other 10%," then it would have served its purpose.

Ultimately, at the very least, this is just an easy, simple way to compile what most of mainstream Protestant Christianity believes. The idea here is that if you're presented with some theological statement, and you're wondering, "Do I believe this?", this book, in some small way, will be a good reference point to compare what you're hearing with what the "average" Christian holds to be true.

Peter admonishes us, "But sanctify the LORD God in your hearts, and always be ready to give a defense to everyone who asks you a reason for the hope that is in you, with meekness and fear…" (1 Peter 3:15)

The phrase "sanctify the LORD God" means "set apart Christ as Lord" in your hearts. Have that settled, He is Lord over your life in all its facets, but always be ready to logically explain with meek humility why you believe what you believe to anyone who asks. This book can partially aid in that endeavor; it offers the scriptural support for the tenet that you can offer as explanation for why you believe it.

I believe the statements contained in this material apply almost universally to every born again, Spirit-filled Christian out there, regardless of your individual sect of Christianity. I believe these confessions are true and correct.

This is my statement of faith, and I hope it's yours too!

THE HOLY BIBLE

Most people—including many who call themselves Christians—think the Bible is simply an historical book, written by people, and therefore, isn't any more accurate or true than, say, Homer's *Odyssey* or Dante's *Inferno*. They think the Bible is a book containing suggestions for patterns of behavior—be nice to your neighbor, don't kill other folks, don't steal, etc.—and most people would say it's overall a good book, except for the super old stuff where God is seemingly a big bully, smiting people left and right, demanding that they kill a bunch of sheep and bulls to appease Him.

Most people reject the Bible to varying levels because it presents a set of "rules" that must be followed in order to be square with God. For example, in modern times, a major sticking point with many folks is God's stance on people who identify as LGBTQ, gender fluid, pansexual, or any other host of terms our society bandies about in an attempt to identify and qualify an "alternative lifestyle."

So while they may accept the statement, "God is love" (1 John 4:8), they reject the statement, "… the law is not made for a righteous person, but for the lawless and insubordinate, for the ungodly and for sinners, for the unholy and profane, for murderers of fathers and murderers of mothers, for manslayers, for fornicators, for sodomites, for kidnappers, for liars, for perjurers, and if there is any other thing that is contrary to sound doctrine…" (1 Timothy 8:9-10)

Since the Bible makes both statements, one must choose whether to accept it at face value (the Bible means what it says; in this instance, sodomy is sin) or pick and choose what pieces of the Bible "fit" with their lifestyle: "Kidnappers are bad, murderers are bad, but homosexuality is not, because all love is good, since God is love and God is good."

(To be clear, I'm not just picking on homosexuals here—notice the above passage of scripture outlines a whole host of sin and lumps fornicators and liars in with sodomites and people who are profane. Sin is sin, in God's eyes.)

Most people accept some of the statements of the Bible as "right" (very few people in the world think coldblooded murder is "okay") but often feel it is antiquated and flawed in view of modern enlightenment concerning science and behavioral studies, dismissing other parts of the Bible as errant. It never applies to everyone equally across the board in their thinking, and most people certainly don't believe it was inspired by God Himself.

However, the Bible demands a response: either this is really from God—all of it—or it isn't. To choose bits and pieces that suit your worldview is simply a form of situational ethics, which opens the entire Book to being dissected into incoherent statements. To use our previous example, this is how we have entire churches of "born again, Spirit-filled" men and women actively practicing homosexuality and thinking "that's okay," because God understands they were made that way. So, the portions of the Bible condemning homosexuality don't apply to them.

When a Christian holds the entire Bible apart from every other book in existence as the *only* Word coming from

God, it directly requires an exercise of faith; it is a decision of the head, a decision of the heart, and a confession of the mouth. What that means is, you accept the Bible as God's Word by an act of faith. If you are sincere in your desire to search and know the Truth, the Holy Spirit, who is the Spirit of Truth, will bear witness in your heart that the Bible is the only true Word of God.

"However, when He, the Spirit of truth, has come, He will guide you into all truth; for He will not speak on His own authority, but whatever He hears He will speak; and He will tell you things to come." (John 16:13)

It is with faith that the majority of mainstream Christianity declares the Bible to be the only inspired, infallible Word of God to mankind, written by men as the Holy Spirit breathed upon them. We believe there is only one gospel, one testament, one Bible, and everything that is outside the printed word of the Bible is open to inspection, even the stuff printed here.

"But even if we, or an angel from heaven, preach any other gospel to you than what we have preached to you, let him be accursed." (Galatians 1:8)

There is no supplementary Word of God, no other additional testament. Books or subsequent "personal revelation" that claim to add further divinely inspired revelation equal to, or greater than, the Scriptures in the canonized Bible are, indeed, not divinely inspired. They are the doctrines of demons (1 Timothy 4:1) or the teachings and traditions of men. (Matthew 15:8-9; Mark 7:8)

Across the board these extraneous "holy words" contradict basic orthodoxy in some way, small or great. Orthodoxy in this context here simply means "authorized and accepted"—what the majority of Christians since the Early Church have held to be as "truth from God."

"But I fear, lest somehow, as the serpent deceived Eve by his craftiness, so your minds may be corrupted from the simplicity that is in Christ. For if he who comes preaches another Jesus whom we have not preached, or if you receive a different spirit which you have not received, or a different gospel which you have not accepted—you may well put up with it!" (2 Corinthians 11:3-4)

Jude makes it clear: "Beloved, while I was very diligent to write to you concerning our common salvation, I found it necessary to write to you exhorting you to contend earnestly for the faith which was once for all delivered to the saints." (Verse 3)

Delivered once and for all. There's nothing that can be added to, or deleted, from the basic Christian orthodoxy of faith without marring the simplicity that is in Christ.

"...the Holy Scriptures, which are able to make you wise for salvation through faith which is in Christ Jesus. All Scripture is given by inspiration of God, and is profitable for doctrine, for reproof, for correction, for instruction in righteousness, that the man of God may be complete, thoroughly equipped for every good work." (2 Timothy 3:15-17)

Inspired in the above passage means "God-breathed." (Strong's #G2315) Christians believe that the Spirit of God inspired the authors of the Bible to write their books. This doesn't mean we believe He "took over" their bodies and moved their hands back and forth across the page like possessed robots. It simply means that what they were writing, in the context of their time, society, and language, originated from God, and therefore is perfect, since God—by definition—must be a perfect Being. (Psalm 18:30)

"…knowing this first, that no prophecy of Scripture is of any private interpretation, for prophecy never came by the will of man, but holy men of God spoke as they were moved by the Holy Spirit." (2 Peter 1:20-21)

This also means, in the original manuscripts, the Bible is inerrant, meaning "without mistakes" or "incapable of being wrong." Every word of it is true and right. The other word we often hear concerning Scripture is "infallible" which has a similar meaning to inerrant, but also is defined as "always effective, incapable of failing." The Word of God never fails when applied in its totality to a person's lifestyle.

"So shall My word be that goes forth from My mouth; it shall not return to Me void, but it shall accomplish what I please, and it shall prosper in the thing for which I sent it." (Isaiah 55:11)

All of this means the earliest findings of the manuscripts that make up the modern Bible are *inspired, infallible and inerrant* (these manuscripts primarily come from the first Dead Sea scrolls, the original excavation, which are among the oldest in existence.) Where minor mistranslations or alternate renderings of a word occur, we believe it does not change the scope and intent of the Bible in its core message: the means by which mankind can approach God and be considered "square" by Him. We shouldn't get hung up on whether or not this particular word in Hebrew means "ostriches" or "jackals." The parts that say "do not commit adultery" are pretty clear in whichever translation you pick up.

I am always asked which translation of the Bible is the correct one. The answer is, nearly all of them. While I may personally believe one translation is a better rendering than another, and yes, there are some translations I find to be woefully inept in omitting canonized verses, just about any copy of the Holy Bible among the major translations you pick up is worth reading and taking by faith as the inspired Word of God directly to you.

I'm old school, so I prefer the original King James. I don't mind all the thee's and thou's. My son prefers the New King James; he believes it has some added clarity to passages of Scripture and is easier to read. Some people like the NIV or the ESV or the NASB. In 99.9% of cases concerning doctrinal disputes, one translation is just as good as another. My suggestion: if you have the means, study all of them. With access to the Internet, you can read probably close to a hundred translations of the Bible for no cost, and they almost invariably always say the exact same thing in intent, even if the word choice is different.

So that all relates to the canonized Scriptures. Later the Gnostic gospels and the books that make up the different categories of Apocrypha were found (many of which were subsequently found among the Dead Sea caves in other nearby excavations after the original findings.) We do not believe these are inspired by God, inerrant and infallible, but that is not to say they are always totally without merit. Many of these extra-scriptural books that are called "Christian" (as opposed to New Age or satanic or Muslim or whatever) and which are widely available, specifically in Catholic and Orthodox circles, are not out-and-out "evil." We simply don't hold them to the same level as canonized scripture, and where there is ever any discrepancy, the sixty-six books overrule all other books, even including this one you're reading right now. Full stop.

Now, again, before you misconstrue that I am pro-extra scriptural writings without question, I want to point out the Gnostic gospels contradict the canonized scripture in many areas—some even teaching an alternate Christ (that He was not preexistent deity, or else denying His humanity—that He did not have a physical flesh body), or denying a literal millennial reign, among other heretical doctrines. Many books in the Apocrypha also contradict the canonized Bible. For example, showing that Jesus had a romantic relationship with Mary the Magdalena, and other such rubbish.

Look, if the Holy Bible is silent on a particular point, then we do not hold something in any other books as "from God" or ultimately, without question, correct. This means good preachers and teachers stick to what the Bible talks about, good students study the Word of God as we have received it in canonized scriptures, and whether or not, for example, the Book of Enoch is correct in naming specific angels is not something to create doctrine around. I urge you, in whatever capacity of ministry you are in, if you can't find proof in the Bible specifically, don't teach it behind the pulpit. That would save about 90% of the trouble we as Christians have concerning doctrinal differences.

The One God

I am very firm in my stance that all true Christians are monotheistic in their beliefs. I went to great lengths in *Aletheia Eleutheroo* outlining how a singular God can manifest as three distinct Persons and still be considered one (numerically) God.

For the purposes of those adhering to Universalistic beliefs, I also believe the one God we as Christians are talking about here is the One whom the Jews call Jehovah or Yahweh. Christians should not believe it is "okay" to call God another name. Not Allah, not Buddha, not Shiva, etc. The Bible makes it very clear there is only one God who revealed His name as "I AM," and that any other gods are false.

"I am the Lord, that is My name; and My glory I will not give to another, nor My praise to carved images." (Isaiah 42:8)

While I know some Buddhists who also claim to be Christians, and I've met people who think when we pray to God, it doesn't matter what name we use because He understands, the Bible demands that we separate God from every other concept of deity out there. There is only one name by which people may be saved, and it is not Mohammed, it is not Vishnu—it is Jesus Christ.

"Nor is there salvation in any other, for there is no other name under heaven given among men by which we must be saved." (Acts 4:12)

I have been asked this question many times over the years: "How do you know Christianity is the 'right' religion?" Assuming someone is just not outright atheistic, and they are searching for "God," when we look at the world's main religions, in my mind, we only have a handful to consider.

Hinduism is polytheistic, with some thirty-six million gods I've been told. (That's a lot!) I've preached to many Hindus who have no trouble adding Jesus Christ to the list of gods they worship; where they struggle is in the phrase, "and I turn away from all other gods, acknowledging Jesus Christ as the only true God."

The same would hold true for any polytheistic religion or Universalist philosophy—if your gods don't care that you're worshipping other gods, then that makes it easy for me to dismiss. I've said it before, that just sounds like *people* to me. And even I, as a human being, wouldn't want to be treated like that. "Doesn't matter if I call him James or Buford or Maynard, it's all the same." Universalism is one of the scariest positions to hold.

I define Universalism as the belief that "all roads lead to God." A universalist life system teaches that whatever you believe, all our concepts of "God" point to the same Being, whether we know Him as Jesus or Allah or Kali, so He is not dogmatic in demanding which religion is right.

I've said in other writings, most people are not sent to hell so much because they're terrible sinners, but rather because they are careless and lazy in their approach to God. What a sad and foolish reason to lose eternal security! Of all the decisions we have to make in this life, certainly "Is there a God, and how do I meet Him?" is the most important.

I am firmly persuaded that God will provide a way for everyone who has ever lived to accept Him and escape eternal judgment. God is not willing that any should perish. (2 Peter 3:8-10) No one will have an excuse for not "knowing" they should have accepted God. No one goes to hell accidentally. If God were to permit that to happen, He would not be just.

Even if a person is an isolated, aboriginal tribe dweller in the most remote jungle on earth, God will provide some way for that person to accept Him. If He has to bring a missionary to witness, or in another case, a person would have read something about the plan of salvation at some point in their lives. They would have heard about the one, true God somewhere, or He would have given them a dream or a vision, an awakening or an angelic visitation. Whatever it takes, everyone who seeks Him will find Him. (Deuteronomy 4:29; Proverbs 8:17; Jeremiah 29:13; Matthew 7:8)

God is just, and people go to hell because they reject Christ. The Father will find a way to enlighten everyone who would try to find Him. God is no respecter of persons. (Acts 10:34; Romans 2:11)

As a brief aside, I have been asked many times over the years about children who die having never had a chance to accept or reject Christ (and understand the consequences of that decision.) Deuteronomy 1:39 speaks of "children, who today have no knowledge of good or evil." Theologians call this the "age of accountability," and it is different for different people, depending on their level of mental understanding. For most people, this is usually around twelve to fourteen years of age, but it can be earlier, or later, or perhaps never at all considering a person of diminished mental capacity.

What I mean by all this is, children and those with mental handicaps who do not possess the ability to understand the plan of salvation do not go to hell when they die, and I reject the concept that they must be baptized into a particular church in order to be "saved" should they die prematurely. There is no Limbo of Infants.

All right then, so moving on in our discourse, take the major monotheistic religions: Judaism, Islam and Christianity. Those are the only three you really have to consider, as they're the only major world religions which maintain, "You must worship only this one God and nothing else."

Technically speaking, I've met many Muslims who are universalist in their faith, just as I've met many Christians and Jews. But the tenets of each of these faiths maintain there is only one God, called either Jehovah or Allah (who are, without question, not the same Being, no matter what you may have heard from modern religious leaders.)

Space fails me here to argue sufficiently why the true religion is not Islam or Judaism, and that's not a cop out— there are hundreds of apologist books written on the subject, mostly written by minds far worthier than mine. As I stated before, I'm not writing to convince an audience, but to an audience that is already convinced. I simply made these statements to briefly answer the question, "Which religion is right?" Basically, you only have to decide between three, because the other ones ultimately don't care who you call God.

To summarize, then, the statement of faith concerning God: We believe that there is ONE God, eternally existent in three distinct Persons: Father, Son, and Holy Spirit, who are all of the same substance, power and worth—exactly equal in every facet, because They are the same Being.

"Go therefore and make disciples of all the nations, baptizing them in the name of the Father and of the Son and of the Holy Spirit..." (Matthew 28:19)

"There is one body and one Spirit, just as you were called in one hope of your calling; one Lord, one faith, one baptism; one God and Father of all, who is above all, and through all, and in you all." (Ephesians 4:4-6)

Exodus 34:5-7 contains the best definition I have found for God, and of course it would be the best, because He gave it of Himself:

"Now the LORD descended in the cloud and stood with him there, and proclaimed the name of the LORD. And the LORD passed before him and proclaimed, 'The LORD, the Lord God, merciful and gracious, longsuffering, and abounding in goodness and truth, keeping mercy for thousands, forgiving iniquity and transgression and sin, by no means clearing the guilty, visiting the iniquity of the fathers upon the children and the children's children to the third and the fourth generation.'"

As a quick side note, I want to point out here that the Bible states no person has seen God the Father. (Exodus 33:20; John 1:18; 5:37; 6:46) Even Moses, the friend of God, only saw His back. I believe it is errant for people to say, "I saw God the Father," when they are describing a vision, in the same sense of how you would see me if we met.

I understand most people mean "I saw the similitude or the glory of God the Father seated on the throne," and many also mean it in a visionary kind of state—their mind's eye, in most cases. However, I believe we should make the distinction.

"I was in heaven, I saw God the Father's face just as if you were seeing me." I do not believe this is biblically accurate.

In the very few instances in my life where I have been blessed to glimpse the throneroom of the Father, I have never seen His form, for He was covered in clouds of glory. There are many verses where the Father enshrouds Himself in clouds. (See Exodus 20:21, 34:5 Numbers 11:25; 2 Samuel 22:12; 2 Chronicles 6:1; Psalm 18:11, as few examples.)

I think we need to make the distinction clearly between, say, seeing the Lord Jesus Christ as opposed to God the Father on the throne. That is not to say people cannot glimpse the *glory* of God on His throne, but I caution everyone who would say, "I have seen the form or face of God the Father." I think that is unscriptural.

Back to the statement of faith, then, God has no beginning, no end, always was before time began, and always will be after time ends. He exists outside of the constraints of the natural existence of time, space and matter, and, being their Creator, has complete control over everything we know to exist in this natural universe. Everything that exists exists through Him; He is above all, surrounds all, and permeates all.

He is both completely immanent (near us) and transcendent (above us.) That is not a contradiction of terms, that is the definition of omnipresence. When we take His transcendence to the extreme over His immanence, we get the erroneous concept of Deism—that there is a God, but He removed Himself from His creation. The other side of that extremity is to downplay God's superiority and holiness (which means "being separate") over everything else in existence. God is your Friend, Brother and Helper; but He is also your Creator, Lord and King.

Everything was created by Him and is upheld by His will.

"For by Him all things were created that are in heaven and that are on earth, visible and invisible, whether thrones or dominions or principalities or powers. All things were created through Him and for Him." (Colossians 1:16)

"…Who [speaking of Jesus] being the brightness of His glory and the express image of His person [God the Father's], and upholding all things by the word of His power, when He had by Himself purged our sins, sat down at the right hand of the Majesty on high…" (Hebrews 1:3 [brackets author's own.])

God, by definition, must be omnipotent (having all power, physically and operationally), omniscient (having all knowledge), and omnipresent (present at all times and all places simultaneously, everywhere and every time at once.) There is nothing more He can learn, nothing can surprise Him. There is nothing He needs to be complete. No outside force can affect or influence Him.

God is holy. (1 Peter 1:15-16) He is love (1 John 4:8)— love is not something He has, it is something He is; love exists because God exists. He is sovereign. (1 Chronicles 29:11-12; Psalm 29:10 and 135:6) God is entirely self-sustained (John 5:26-27), needing nothing from no one ever. This does not mean He does not have desires, hopes and expectations, but He doesn't *need* anything from anyone. He is the only self-existent Being, something wholly unique to Himself. If everything else ceased to be, He would still be. God is unchangeable. (Malachi 3:6) We call this immutability and invariability. He cannot alter His existence nor character in any way.

God is just, righteous, compassionate and merciful. (Deuteronomy 32:4; Psalm 25:8-14, 86:15 and 89:14; Mark 6:34; Romans 3:25-26) He is also jealous and an all-consuming fire. (Exodus 34:14 and 20:5; Deuteronomy 4:24; Hebrews 12:29)

God is also wrathful, full of anger against sin because of His holiness and love of righteousness. It is wrong to say that the God represented in the Old Testament is different than the God represented in the New Testament. If He was wrathful in ancient times, He is wrathful still. (Jeremiah 30:23; Nahum 1:2; Romans 1:18; Revelation 19:15)

The difference, therefore, between the Old Testament and the New Testament is not that God has changed in the slightest. "For I am the LORD, I do not change..." (Malachi 3:6) Rather, God has provided a way to save us from His own wrath through the permanent and complete sin offering of His Son, the Lord Jesus Christ.

This means that God the Father poured out His wrath upon Jesus Christ (who is very God Himself), taking the place for us, so that we do not have to be the ones to receive it. Jesus took the punishment upon Himself for our mistakes.

This, right here, is the entire crux of Christian belief. Not that Jesus was a nice guy and a good prophet. But that He was God Himself, who took our place for the punishment of sin. And this, more than any other thing, proves to me that Christianity is the "real" religion. No other religion offers such an amazing, mind-blowing gift of self-sacrifice. No other god comes close to doing this in any other religion of the world.

Jesus Christ

Jesus declared, "...I and My Father are one." (John 10:30) So the people who claim that Jesus never said He was God are completely wrong. "...Most assuredly, I say to you, before Abraham was, I AM." (John 8:58) This is why the Jewish leaders of His day sought to kill Him. He most certainly said, "I am God." All of His actions corroborated His statements. So, all of humanity is confronted with a decision to make: either He was telling the truth, or He was a complete lunatic. There is no middle ground. His claim demands a response.

Therefore, we believe in the deity of the Lord Jesus Christ. He is God, the only One, the same God as the Father and the Holy Spirit, the eternal, co-existent, consubstantial, all-powerful, all-knowing, always present God.

"In the beginning was the Word, and the Word was with God, and the Word was God. He was in the beginning with God. All things were made through Him, and without Him nothing was made that was made. In Him was life, and the life was the light of men... And the Word became flesh and dwelt among us, and we beheld His glory, the glory as of the only begotten of the Father, full of grace and truth." (John 1:1-4, 14)

When we pray to the Lᴏʀᴅ God, we are praying to Jehovah, from whom Jesus proceeds, of the same co-equal substance and worth as the Father and the Holy Spirit. Jesus is *not* a third God. However, He can be perceived as distinct from the other two Persons of the Godhead.

Now, before we get any further into the statement of faith concerning the Lord Jesus Christ, I want to take a brief aside to outline a very important concept. One of the primary reasons for writing this book was to address the following problem: "With so many voices in the world today—so many preachers, so many theology books—how can I know that what I'm hearing (or reading) is coming from people who are 'rightly dividing the word of truth'?"

"Study to shew thyself approved unto God, a workman that needeth not to be ashamed, rightly dividing the word of truth." (2 Timothy 2:15)

One of the key factors in "rightly dividing" is found in the hermeneutical process called Christocentrism—that is, Christ is the center, the entire *point* of the Bible. Everything you read in the printed Word is to be interpreted through the actions and teachings of Jesus as presented in the four Gospels. We are supposed to study the Word that is personified in Jesus Christ. (And ergo, all subsequent teaching is to be interpreted through Him, who is the Word.)

As the above passage in John 1:1 states, Jesus *is* the Word of God. That word "Word" (*smile*) means the "entire will of God—His commandments, His decrees, His expectations, His complete thought process toward humanity—is summed up in Jesus Christ."

When we accept the truth that Jesus is the Word incarnate (made flesh), we then have to accept that Jesus was the will of God in action. He is the only perfect and complete expression of God's will being made manifest upon the earth. He only did that which He saw His Father doing. (John 5:19) So that means everything we read or see or hear should be interpreted through the lens of "What Would Jesus Do, Teach or Say?"

When listening to or reading any doctrine from anyone, we must ask ourselves this question: "Is what I'm hearing or reading or seeing in accordance with the *example* and *teaching* of Jesus Christ?" Secondly, and equally important, "Would Jesus have functioned in the manner being presented to me?" Is the person sharing this information acting as Jesus would have acted?

This would solve the vast, vast majority of the weird theology that is out there today. If it doesn't line up to what Jesus *did* and what Jesus *said*, it needs to be dismissed as errant.

As an aside to this aside, I would like to propose a question to you, dear reader: When will Jesus be presented to the multitudes of "today" as He was presented to the multitudes of "yesterday" in His earthly ministry?

Chew on that, precious people!

So, moving on in the statement of faith, we believe that God came down to earth and took on the form of a Man. He was born of a virgin, named Mary, conceived supernaturally and miraculously when the Holy Spirit overshadowed her, and she was found with Child, having never known a man. (Matthew 1:18, 23) The blood that was in Jesus' body was specially created by the Spirit, untainted by sin. (1 Peter 1:18-19), but He was born of a completely human mother.

This makes Jesus Christ both fully God and fully Man inside the same human body. Theologians call this the "hypostatic union." Jesus was not a demigod, half-man, half-god; He was not a hybrid species or alien. He was perfectly human, while at the same time remaining perfectly God, because God cannot change His nature. Jesus did not stop being God while He was contained in the human body.

Since Jesus is fully God, He is incapable of making a mistake. As God, He cannot sin, and He never sinned at any point in His life on this earth. He never lied, He never stole, He never cheated, He never lusted, He never envied or coveted. He never thought an evil thought, nor spoke an evil word. He never hated anyone, nor wished them harm. He never thought up evil on His own.

"For He made Him who knew no sin to be sin for us, that we might become the righteousness of God in Him." (2 Corinthians 5:21)

This does not mean He could never be angry or sad, but it does mean that His emotions never ruled over His mind and spirit. Because He had a physical body just like yours and mine, He could become hungry or tired—but He was never sick, because sickness is a result of sin and death (Mark 2:1-10; John 5:1-15; Romans 5:12; 1 Corinthians 15:21), and Jesus was without sin.

Since He was also fully human, He could be tested and tempted by sin or evil coming from the outside against Him. In His humanity, He was tempted in exactly the same ways that we are tempted (Hebrews 4:15), but because of the hypostatic union, He was wholly able to resist it. (Matthew 4:1-11; Luke 4:1-13) This means, it takes God living inside of mankind to allow man to be holy before God. There is no other way, no work or ritual a person can perform to be consider "righteous." No one can do it on their own. We call this experience of God living inside a person being "born again." (John 3:3)

To sum this all up, I believe Jesus could not be tempted in His deity, but He could be tempted in His humanity. The debate of whether or not Jesus "could" have actually sinned is extraneous to the bedrock statement that Jesus did *not* sin, one time, ever. He perfectly followed God the Father's will at all times.

Jesus Christ performed supernatural miracles while on this earth, healing people of every kind of sickness and disease. (Matthew 4:23) He controlled the weather, commanding a storm on the sea to abate. (Mark 4:39) He had total authority over natural creation, changing water to wine (John 2:1-11), commanding a corrupted fig tree to wither. (Matthew 21:19) He had total authority over the demonic. (Luke 8:26-29) He prophesied with perfect accuracy one hundred percent of the time. (Matthew 24 and 26:34; Mark 9:30-32)

However, we believe that He did all of these works not as God, but as Man. The reason for this distinction is that Jesus as a Man was anointed by God the Father with the Holy Spirit's power. (Acts 10:38) The word *Christ* is a title meaning "Anointed One." (Strong's #G5547) The purpose of this anointing was to provide a prime Example for His believers to follow: that we, too, could do the same supernatural works as He, through delegated authority in His name. (John 14:12-14)

Like I stated before, prior to being born as a Baby through Mary, Jesus was called "the Word," or we could render it as the "Complete Thought or Expression" of God. (Strong's #G3056) The Word did not stop being God (John 1:1, 14), rather He set aside His rights and sovereign privilege to act as God while physically on the earth. (Philippians 2:7)

Theologians call this the *kenosis* of God. The phrase "made Himself of no reputation" in Philippians 2 is the Greek word *kenoo* (Strong's #G2758), which means He "emptied" Himself, and chose to limit Himself to one physical body, in one location, in one moment of time, becoming reliant upon the power of the Holy Spirit to act supernaturally. (Luke 3:21-23; 4:14)

He did this to show humanity that when a person is completely submitted to God, they can do anything that is in line with God's character and nature. (Philippians 4:13)

After His earthly ministry (a period of about three years) Jesus was arrested and condemned to death via crucifixion on a cross. (Matthew 27:32-56)

Therefore, we believe that Jesus Christ died a physical death, in the same manner than any other human being would perish by being nailed to a cross. It is a real occurrence that even most non-Christian scholars attest to happening.

"Let this mind be in you which was also in Christ Jesus, who, being in the form of God, did not consider it robbery to be equal with God, but made Himself of no reputation, taking the form of a bondservant, and coming in the likeness of men. And being found in appearance as a man, He humbled Himself and became obedient to the point of death, even the death of the cross. Therefore God also has highly exalted Him and given Him the name which is above every name, that at the name of Jesus every knee should bow, of those in heaven, and of those on earth, and of those under the earth, and that every tongue should confess that Jesus Christ is Lord, to the glory of God the Father." (Philippians 2:5-11)

After His physical death, His spirit entered into the realm of the dead, where He remained three days. There is quite a bit of contention concerning this concept, with Catholics and a host of varying Protestant faiths adhering to numerous interpretations of certain scriptures concerning what happened to Jesus Christ after He died.

I believe that Jesus' spirit descended into Sheol/Hades (Strong's #H7585 and #G86) to the place called Abraham's Bosom (Luke 16:19-31), sometimes referred to as Paradise when used as a distinct place from Heaven (the realm of God the Father.) Prior to Christ's death, Abraham's Bosom is where the righteous dead went, as opposed to the unrighteous dead, who went to Hell proper, the place of eternal torment.

We'll discuss Heaven/Hell in the section on Eternity, but for now, since Jesus was a righteous Jew, He would not have been sent to Hell to be tormented, any more than would Abraham, Moses or Elisha.

So while in Abraham's Bosom, Jesus showed the righteous dead who had passed away before Him that He was the prophesied Messiah of the Old Testament, very God Himself. After which, their faith in Him would release them to enter Heaven. I believe Ephesians 4:8-10 is speaking about this occurrence. (This also means I do not believe there is anyone righteous in the bowels of the earth any longer, that Abraham's Bosom is "empty.")

What was the point of Jesus Christ's literal death? To atone, or "make payment," for our sins vicariously, once and for all, before God the Father.

"For the life of the flesh is in the blood, and I have given it to you upon the altar to make atonement for your souls; for it is the blood that makes atonement for the soul." (Leviticus 17:11)

God requires a blood sacrifice for the forgiveness of sins—the innocent must stand in place for the guilty. In the Old Testament, the blood of sheep and bulls covered the sins of the believing Jews. However, this was not a permanent solution, since they're just animals bound to the same earthly principles that we are. Animal sacrifice in the Old Testament was a type and foreshadowing of Jesus Christ, the Lamb of God Himself, being slain. (John 1:29; Revelation 13:8)

"Sacrifice and offering You did not desire, but a body You have prepared for Me. In burnt offerings and sacrifices for sin You had no pleasure. Then I said, 'Behold, I have come—in the volume of the book it is written of Me—to do Your will, O God.'" (Hebrews 10:5-7)

Hebrews 9:22 (and Leviticus 17:11 again) state that without the shedding of blood, there is no forgiveness of sins. By shedding His perfect, sinless blood on the cross, Jesus made atonement for all sins. Here are a bunch of verses talking about the blood of Jesus:

"...For all have sinned and fall short of the glory of God, being justified freely by His grace through the redemption that is in Christ Jesus, whom God set forth as a propitiation by His blood, through faith, to demonstrate His righteousness, because in His forbearance God had passed over the sins that were previously committed..." (Romans 3:23-25)

"Much more then, having now been justified by His blood, we shall be saved from wrath through Him." (Romans 5:9)

"In Him we have redemption through His blood, the forgiveness of sins, according to the riches of His grace..." (Ephesians 1:7)

"...So Christ was offered once to bear the sins of many. To those who eagerly wait for Him He will appear a second time, apart from sin, for salvation." (Hebrews 9:28)

"...Who Himself bore our sins in His own body on the tree, that we, having died to sins, might live for righteousness—by whose stripes you were healed." (1 Peter 2:24)

"But if we walk in the light as He is in the light, we have fellowship with one another, and the blood of Jesus Christ His Son cleanses us from all sin." (1 John 1:7)

So the crux of all human history led to the crucifixion of Jesus. Since that point in history, we are now in the time of grace, and salvation is free to any and all who would call upon the name of the Lord, put their trust in His atoning blood, confess their sins and repent—which means to "to express sincere regret and remorse"—turn away from the world in their lifestyle, and accept His free gift of salvation.

Now, back to the narrative, three days after Jesus Christ was entombed, He was raised from the dead. (Matthew 17:23)

"For I delivered to you first of all that which I also received: that Christ died for our sins according to the Scriptures, and that He was buried, and that He rose again the third day according to the Scriptures…" (1 Corinthians 15:3-4)

The purpose of Jesus Christ's death was to atone (make payment, restitution) for all of the sins of mankind, once and for all. The purpose of Jesus Christ's resurrection was to prove His authority over those sins, and death in all its facets—which is the result of sin. (Romans 6:23) The resurrection proves the validity of Jesus saying, "I can forgive all your sins," because He defeated sin and death, being glorified by God the Father.

"Men of Israel, hear these words: Jesus of Nazareth, a Man attested by God to you by miracles, wonders, and signs which God did through Him in your midst, as you yourselves also know—Him, being delivered by the determined purpose and foreknowledge of God, you have taken by lawless hands, have crucified, and put to death; whom God raised up, having loosed the pains of death, because it was not possible that He should be held by it." (Acts 2:22-24)

His spirit re-entered His physical body, which was not corrupted in any form. (Acts 2:27) Jesus' body was changed into His resurrected (we call this "glorified") body. (Philippians 3:20-21; 1 Corinthians 15:42-44) It is still indeed a human body (Luke 24:39), but is no longer constrained to physical earthly limitations (it doesn't grow old, break down, get tired, etc.)

I want to emphasize this point: just as Jesus Christ did not cease to be God when He became Man; likewise, He will not cease to be Man throughout eternity as He remains God. He is forever linked with Adam's race. For the rest of eternity, Jesus Christ will be "tied" to that glorified body, thereby making a Bridge between God and mankind, the Firstborn of many brethren. (Romans 8:29)

This, to me, is the greatest expression of LOVE ever displayed, that not only would He die for us (John 15:13), but that God of very God would *become* One of us for all eternity. No other religion in the world offers this profound sacrifice, thereby further showing me that Christianity is the "right" religion.

Christians believe that after a forty-day period of time, in which the resurrected Christ was seen by many, He ascended back into Heaven.

"…Who also said, 'Men of Galilee, why do you stand gazing up into heaven? This same Jesus, who was taken up from you into heaven, will so come in like manner as you saw Him go into heaven.'" (Acts 1:11)

"Who is he who condemns? It is Christ who died, and furthermore is also risen, who is even at the right hand of God, who also makes intercession for us." (Romans 8:34)

"God, who at various times and in various ways spoke in time past to the fathers by the prophets, has in these last days spoken to us by His Son, whom He has appointed heir of all things, through whom also He made the worlds; who being the brightness of His glory and the express image of His person, and upholding all things by the word of His power, when He had by Himself purged our sins, sat down at the right hand of the Majesty on high, having become so much better than the angels, as He has by inheritance obtained a more excellent name than they." (Hebrews 1:1-4)

The present-day ministry of Jesus Christ is a vital truth to Christians now. Seated at the right hand of God the Father, our Lord lives forever to make intercession on our behalves. (Hebrews 7:25) What's fantastic about this truth is that Jesus *always* has His prayers answered because the Father loves the Son and honors His intercession because Jesus always does the things that are pleasing to the Father. (John 3:35; 8:29) He is our merciful and faithful High Priest.

"Therefore, in all things He had to be made like His brethren, that He might be a merciful and faithful High Priest in things pertaining to God, to make propitiation for the sins of the people." (Hebrews 2:17)

Jesus is the Author and Finisher (or Perfecter) of our faith. (Hebrews 12:2) It is because of this present-day ministry of the Lord that we, also, enter into all the grace and power of the Father that Jesus is in. It enables us to keep His commandments and do the things that are pleasing in His sight, therefore, we receive from Him whatever we ask as well. (1 John 3:22)

The Lord is the Apostle of our confession. (Hebrews 3:1) The blood of Jesus applied to the Mercy Seat in heaven allows

Him to be our Mediator of this new covenant before God the Father, who is the Judge of all.

"But you have come to Mount Zion and to the city of the living God, the heavenly Jerusalem, to an innumerable company of angels, to the general assembly and church of the firstborn who are registered in heaven, to God the Judge of all, to the spirits of just men made perfect, to Jesus the Mediator of the new covenant, and to the blood of sprinkling that speaks better things than that of Abel." (Hebrews 12:22-24)

We need nothing else and no one else to plead our cases— in whatever situation we may face—before the Father, except the blood of Jesus. We do not need to "convince" God of anything, because Jesus has already fulfilled every element of the Father's need for justice against sin, and now we have His mercy. We only have to appropriate those promises through faith, and our entreaties are granted upon the basis of Jesus being our High Priest and Apostle.

Christians believe that Jesus Christ will physically return again in power and glory. This is called the "Second Coming" or "Second Advent." It marks the end of this age. Jesus is returning to judge the living and the dead. All who believe in Him will return with Him to Heaven. Those who do not believe in Him will enter into everlasting, and literal, damnation. (This means I do not believe in the annihilation of souls. I take Mark 9:48 to mean eternal punishment.)

To close out this segment, the following are several verses on the Second Coming of Christ:

"For the Son of Man will come in the glory of His Father with His angels, and then He will reward each according to his works." (Matthew 16:27)

"This is the will of the Father who sent Me, that of all He has given Me I should lose nothing, but should raise it up at the last day. And this is the will of Him who sent Me, that everyone who sees the Son and believes in Him may have everlasting life; and I will raise him up at the last day." (John 6:39-40)

"Let not your heart be troubled; you believe in God, believe also in Me. In My Father's house are many mansions; if it were not so, I would have told you. I go to prepare a place for you. And if I go and prepare a place for you, I will come again and receive you to Myself; that where I am, there you may be also." (John 14:1-3)

"For the Lord Himself will descend from heaven with a shout, with the voice of an archangel, and with the trumpet of God. And the dead in Christ will rise first. Then we who are alive and remain shall be caught up together with them in the clouds to meet the Lord in the air. And thus we shall always be with the Lord." (1 Thessalonians 4:16-17)

"...Looking for the blessed hope and glorious appearing of our great God and Savior Jesus Christ..." (Titus 2:13)

"But the day of the Lord will come as a thief in the night, in which the heavens will pass away with a great noise, and the elements will melt with fervent heat; both the earth and the works that are in it will be burned up." (2 Peter 3:10)

"...And behold, I am coming quickly, and My reward is with Me, to give to every one according to his work." (Revelation 22:12)

THE HOLY SPIRIT

The third Person in the Trinity is the Holy Spirit. He is co-equal with God the Father, the Creator, and God the Son, Jesus Christ. They are the same numerically one God. The Spirit is of the same substance and worth, and when we pray to God, we pray to the Holy Spirit, just as we pray to the Father and the Son. They cannot be separated or divided, but They can be perceived as distinct.

To deny one Person of the Godhead is to deny all. We cannot say, "I believe in Jehovah, and not Jesus Christ," and be considered "right" before God. Nor can we say, "I believe in Jesus, but I do not believe in the Holy Spirit." To accept Jesus Christ as God is to accept the Holy Spirit as the same God, just as the Father.

Now, there is doctrinal dispute between Trinitarian and nontrinitarian Christians on the Person of God. I believe some sects of nontrinitarian Christianity are heretical, borderline cults; however, my issues with those groups usually go beyond just nontrinitarian theology. There are other doctrines that cause me to call them "incorrect" over and above just the varying definitions of nontrinitarianism.

Briefly, the primary definitions of nontrinitarianism are: binitarianism (two deities in one Person, or else two separate deities); dynamic Monarchianism (also called "adoptionism;"

there is only one Person within God, and Jesus was "made" God by the Father either at His baptism or ascension), with its offshoot of modal Monarchianism (one God in three "modes" of operation as the Father, the Son and the Holy Spirit); or Unitarianism (one God in one Person, which denies the deity of Jesus Christ.)

Now, I have met many wonderful Oneness Pentecostals who are truly born again and filled with the Spirit, and while I disagree with their philosophy concerning the Oneness of God, it's never prevented fellowship or co-ministry.

I spend a sizeable portion of *Aletheia Eleutheroo* outlining why I believe in a Trinitarian, though numerically singular, God, for people who adhere to a Oneness theology, if they are so inclined to read it. I'll state it again: Christianity is a monotheistic religion, even though I believe the one, true God is represented in three Persons eternally.

Continuing on, then, the Spirit is not an impersonal Being—some "force" like wind or fire, even though He is described this way in the Bible. He is not an "it." He possesses exactly the same attributes as the Godhead, meaning He possesses emotions and a voice and a spirit body, just as God the Father. He speaks, and He can become angry, joyful, grieved, etc. (See 1 Samuel 11:6; Isaiah 63:10; Luke 10:21; Acts 13:2 for just a few examples.)

Nearly all people who call themselves Christians believe in the ministry of the Holy Spirit today, that He is present during salvation and baptizes the believer into the body of Christ (the Church), enabling him or her to live a godly, righteous lifestyle.

"Jesus answered, 'Most assuredly, I say to you, unless one is born of water and the Spirit, he cannot enter the kingdom of God. That which is born of the flesh is flesh, and that which is born of the Spirit is spirit. Do not marvel that I said to you, "You must be born again." The wind blows where it wishes, and you hear the sound of it, but cannot tell where it comes from and where it goes. So is everyone who is born of the Spirit.'" (John 3:5-8)

In fact, it is biblical truth that without the Holy Spirit there can be no regeneration. (Titus 3:4-7) Just as He was present at the birth of creation (Genesis 1:2), He is present at the new birth.

"But you are not in the flesh but in the Spirit, if indeed the Spirit of God dwells in you. Now if anyone does not have the Spirit of Christ, he is not His." (Romans 8:9)

It takes the Holy Spirit residing within the spirit of a believer in order to perceive the spiritual things of God. Naturally minded man is incapable of receiving spiritual truth, apart from the Holy Spirit, because he perceives them as "foolishness," archaic, mystical, and unscientific, as unnatural as magic and Santa Claus.

"But the natural man does not receive the things of the Spirit of God, for they are foolishness to him; nor can he know them, because they are spiritually discerned." (1 Corinthians 2:14)

Therefore, without the indwelling of the Spirit—the "born again" experience—mankind is incapable of walking correctly before the Lord, being led solely by our flesh, which includes our minds, wills and emotions as well as our bodies. We are primarily driven by basic needs and selfish wants, usually with very little left over for our fellow human beings. And while most of us are not psychopathic murderers or violent thieves, we all know of times where we have placed our wants and desires over the needs of another.

No matter how we strive to be a "good person," we will fail at some time in our own strength, doing things we know deep down are wrong, and perhaps we don't even wish to do them—but we cannot stop ourselves.

"I say then: Walk in the Spirit, and you shall not fulfill the lust of the flesh. For the flesh lusts against the Spirit, and the Spirit against the flesh; and these are contrary to one another, so that you do not do the things that you wish. But if you are led by the Spirit, you are not under the law." (Galatians 5:16-18)

After we are born again by the Holy Spirit and our faith in the salvation of Jesus Christ, we are not suddenly "perfected" outwardly in every thought and deed. Our spirits are made perfect toward God, but we must "crucify our flesh" natures, choosing to follow the precepts of God as opposed to our own desires. This becomes a lifetime process of yielding to the Holy Spirit within us, bearing His good fruit (Galatians 5:22-26) while denying the works of the flesh. (Galatians 5:19-21)

Throughout our Christian walk as we mature in our relationship with Jesus Christ and grow in our understanding, the Holy Spirit teaches us the way God expects us to behave in thought and action. Of course, we will all have setbacks and shortcomings, but the primary goal of every born-again Christian is, "That I might know Him..." in an ever-increasing relationship. (Philippians 3:10) The Holy Spirit teaches us the way of Christ and separates fallacy from truth. (John 14:26; 16:13)

"As you therefore have received Christ Jesus the Lord, so walk in Him, rooted and built up in Him and established in the faith, as you have been taught, abounding in it with thanksgiving. Beware lest anyone cheat you through philosophy and empty deceit, according to the tradition of men, according to the basic principles of the world, and not according to Christ. For in Him dwells all the fullness of the Godhead bodily; and you are complete in Him, who is the head of all principality and power." (Colossians 2:6-10)

Jesus, at His ascension, commanded that believers be baptized in the name of the Father, the Son and the Holy Spirit. (Matthew 28:19) Catholics and Protestants alike, nearly across the board, believe this. This baptism unto salvation is usually accompanied by some form of water baptism, as an outward declaration of what the Christian believes has happened internally.

Many of the Protestant denominations, especially the Baptists, and nearly all Pentecostal, charismatic Christians, believe in full water immersion (Matthew 3:16); some denominations, primarily Lutheran and Methodist (there are exceptions, of course), only in sprinkling with water as in the Catholic tradition.

I believe water baptism is an important doctrine, outwardly symbolizing the regeneration of the spirit inwardly. It is a public declaration that the person being baptized has claimed Jesus Christ as their Lord and Savior, separating themselves to Him only for the remainder of their lives.

I do not believe that water baptism in and of itself makes you "saved," nor does it cleanse one's sins—only the blood of Jesus does that. (again, 1 John 1:7) Still, water baptism is an important part in the Holy Spirit's inward work of regeneration. What happens in water baptism is the beginning of the process that cuts away old lifestyle patterns, the crucifying of the flesh—that is, the body, the mind, and the soulish emotions. This process continues throughout one's life in Christ Jesus.

"Then Peter said to them, 'Repent, and let every one of you be baptized in the name of Jesus Christ for the remission of sins; and you shall receive the gift of the Holy Spirit. For the promise is to you and to your children, and to all who are afar off, as many as the Lord our God will call.'" (Acts 2:38-39)

So, to continue, after Jesus Christ ascended, the Holy Spirit came upon the disciples and filled them, so that they spoke with other tongues.

"And they were all filled with the Holy Spirit and began to speak with other tongues, as the Spirit gave them utterance." (Acts 2:4)

Spirit-filled Christians—and by that, I mean mostly those who call themselves Pentecostal or charismatic—take baptism a step further and believe there is an infilling of the Holy Spirit as a separate occurrence after salvation that further equips the person to minister supernaturally.

Why we believe there is a second baptism is explained in Acts 2. This was after Jesus had breathed upon them and said, "Receive the Holy Spirit." (John 20:22) So why did He tell them to wait for the coming of the Spirit, if He had already given them the Spirit earlier? This shows a progression: John 20:22 is when the disciples became born again; Acts 2:4 is when they were filled with the Holy Spirit.

The baptism of the Holy Spirit, with the evidence of speaking in tongues, also called a "heavenly prayer language," is given to believers so they might be empowered to bear witness of the truth of Jesus Christ's gospel. It is a sign to unbelievers. (1 Corinthians 14:20-25)

"But you shall receive power when the Holy Spirit has come upon you; and you shall be witnesses to Me in

Jerusalem, and in all Judea and Samaria, and to the end of the earth." (Acts 1:8)

The primary sign of being filled with the Holy Spirit is an empowering boldness to share the truth of Jesus Christ with the world. Boldness to declare the Word of the Lord, and boldness to step out in faith to see the miraculous manifested upon humanity's needs.

"And when they had prayed, the place where they were assembled together was shaken; and they were all filled with the Holy Spirit, and they spoke the word of God with boldness." (Acts 4:31)

The secondary sign (but equally important) of being filled with the Spirit is the evidence of speaking in tongues. The section entitled "Tongues" in *Overwhelmed by the Spirit* goes into a lot of detail concerning this truth. I believe in speaking in tongues, and that it is vitally important in the day-to-day life of the Christian, enabling us to live a holy lifestyle; but also to administer the anointing of the Holy Spirit to others, in the name of signs, wonders, miracles, spiritual gifts, healing, prophetic utterance, and so on. (1 Corinthians 12:1-11) Speaking in tongues releases the power of the Holy Spirit in our lives and the lives of those we come in contact with. I do not apologize for being a "tongue talker."

Just as Jesus Christ was anointed with the Holy Spirit and power (Acts 10:38), we too are anointed to act in the same authority He had over sickness, disease, poverty in all its facets, and the demonic. It is the Spirit's modern-day ministry that enables the Christian to do all these things through His delegated authority and power.

"For we do not wrestle against flesh and blood, but against principalities, against powers, against the rulers of the darkness of this age, against spiritual hosts of wickedness in the heavenly places." (Ephesians 6:12)

The present-day ministry of the Holy Spirit is a vital truth we hold. Through the indwelling and infilling of the Holy Spirit, especially with the evidence of speaking in tongues, we believe that He helps us overcome our mental, emotional, and physical weaknesses or infirmities—our frailties as human beings.

"And I will pray the Father, and He will give you another Helper, that He may abide with you forever—the Spirit of truth, whom the world cannot receive, because it neither sees Him nor knows Him; but you know Him, for He dwells with you and will be in you." (John 14:16)

Jesus called the Spirit another "Helper." That word is *Parakletos* in Greek (Strong's #G3875), and means "Comforter, Advocate." A legal term, it means one called alongside to plead our case.

"However, when He, the Spirit of truth, has come, He will guide you into all truth; for He will not speak on His own authority, but whatever He hears He will speak; and He will tell you things to come." (John 16:13)

Because He is the Spirit of truth, He reveals *the* "Truth" (which is Jesus Christ as the Word of God incarnate—remember, that means the complete Thought of God toward mankind.) It is the Truth that you know which sets you free, and we are sanctified (set apart) by that Truth. (John 8:32; 17:17)

"Likewise the Spirit also helps in our weaknesses. For we do not know what we should pray for as we ought, but the Spirit Himself makes intercession for us with groanings which cannot be uttered." (Romans 8:26)

This is all the present-day ministry of the Holy Spirit. He helps us to arrogate and claim our rights under the blood of Jesus to take authority, in His name, against our circumstances and infirmity.

Now, as a segue into the next chapter, here seems a good place to put in some statements concerning God's delegated authority to His children and the current world system.

The Bible teaches that heaven and the highest heavens (the sky and the cosmos), as well as the earth and all it contains, belong to the LORD. (Deuteronomy 10:14; Psalms 24:1) However, God turned over the stewardship of the earth to Adam and Eve. (Genesis 1:28) Mankind became the caretaker of the world system with operational authority and dominion delegated to it by God.

When Adam and Eve sinned, that authority to control the world system was turned over to Satan. The Bible calls him the "prince and power of the air" (Ephesians 2:2) and the "god of this world," or "age." (2 Corinthians 4:4)

This is why bad things happen in a world God calls "very good." (Genesis 1:31) Many people use this as a reason to deny God's existence, or rebel against Him: "If God's so good, why does He allow *insert some horrible tragedy here* to happen?"

However, this is not a valid reason to reject Him. God in His sovereignty, as the Possessor of heaven and earth, has permitted mankind to choose to turn over their delegated authority to Satan and his demons. And that is the sole reason why tragedy, death, disease, war, famine, pestilence, earthquakes, floods and any other "bad thing" happens.

But the good news is, when Jesus was crucified and raised from the dead, He took the keys of death and hell. (Revelation 1:18) Reference Matthew 16:13-19; these keys represent the operational power and authority to bind and loose, lock and unlock, permit and deny.

Colossians 2:15 says He triumphed over those principalities and powers, making a public spectacle of them, depriving them of their power over people who would put their faith and trust in Him. God causes *us* to triumph in Christ. (2 Corinthians 2:14)

All authority (the power of absolute rule) is given to Him. (Matthew 28:18) And He in turn has given it to those who believe in Him and call upon His name for salvation. Reference Psalm 91.

"And He said to them, 'I saw Satan fall like lightning from heaven. Behold, I give you the authority to trample on serpents and scorpions, and over all the power of the enemy, and nothing shall by any means hurt you. Nevertheless do not rejoice in this, that the spirits are subject to you, but rather rejoice because your names are written in heaven.'" (Luke 10:18-20)

The Depravity of Man

There are a lot of ethics debates centering on the question of "Is man inherently good or evil or neutral?" The Bible states very clearly that there is no neutrality concerning Jesus Christ. (Matthew 12:30; Luke 11:23) We cannot claim neutrality when it comes to the Bible and its declarations. That is not an excuse we can give to God when we die.

Neither does the Bible leave any gray area concerning the inherent state of mankind, from the moment one is first conceived in the womb. (Psalm 51:5) This doctrine is called "Original Sin." This specific phrase is not used in the Bible, but the principle is very much biblical: that a) every human being on this planet is guilty of sin before God by their own actions (no one has acted perfectly in line with God's commandments, save Jesus Christ) and b) everyone has inherited from their parents a nature that is deadened toward God, corrupted by the sin principle. (Romans 5:12)

This does not mean that every person on the planet wants to be a violent marauder, a liar, a thief, an "evil" man or woman. Most people want to do good things, to whatever definition of "good" they happen to have.

But the problem is people have no universal definition of "good." From their standpoint, technically speaking, Nazi Germany thought they were doing the right thing. Many

Puritans thought the witch trials were correct. Even the papacy at the time thought the Crusades were what God wanted.

The Bible makes it very clear: "There is none righteous, no, not one; there is none who understands; there is none who seeks after God. They have all turned aside; they have together become unprofitable; there is none who does good, no, not one... for all have sinned and fall short of the glory of God, being justified freely by His grace through the redemption that is in Christ Jesus..." (Romans 3:11-12, 23-24)

The vast majority of Christianity, Catholic or Protestant, accepts this to be true, though in recent years I have seen and heard a few alarming statements that seem to question the validity of humanity's inherent depravity. Many times, these statements are made in the context of hypergrace or extreme sovereignty of God movements.

I believe that all people without exception are guilty of sin, no matter how "slight," and face the judgment of God. Take the kindest nicest, sweetest old lady who does nothing all day but feed the homeless, care for orphans and give shelter to lost puppies and kittens—she at some point in time, by word, thought or deed, has done something against God's decrees. According to James 2:10, if she is guilty in one aspect against the law, she is guilty of it all.

"If we say that we have no sin, we deceive ourselves, and the truth is not in us. If we confess our sins, He is faithful and just to forgive us our sins and to cleanse us from all unrighteousness. If we say that we have not sinned, we make Him a liar, and His word is not in us." (1 John 1:8-10)

Sin separates us from God. Because He is a holy God—which is the universal definition of "good"—He cannot have relationship with sin. This may sound very "black and white," and it is. One of the few things God is incapable of doing is associating Himself to sin.

"But your iniquities have separated you from your God; and your sins have hidden His face from you, so that He will not hear." (Isaiah 59:2)

When Adam sinned, God needed a way to reestablish connection to him and yet still remain completely holy. This is not to say that God had nothing to do with mankind after Adam and Eve fell. It just means that God's Spirit could no longer reside in Adam and Eve's (and all future generations) spirits. So after the Fall of mankind, before Christ's crucifixion, God could only deal with humanity externally.

The question, then, was how could God fully reconcile mankind to Himself and still remain holy? How could He settle His demand for justice against a guilty creation who had rebelled against His decrees, and not wholly destroy that creation with a justified punishment?

The answer: take that punishment upon Himself. The innocent would stand in place for the guilty. This is why He demands that we acknowledge Jesus Christ as the only Way of salvation, because it is His master plan and it cost Him so much to procure.

"Then He said to them, "Thus it is written, and thus it was necessary for the Christ to suffer and to rise from the dead the third day, and that repentance and remission of sins should be preached in His name to all nations, beginning at Jerusalem."' (Luke 24:46-47)

Again, this is another proof to me that Christianity is the correct religion. Other religions are about what you can do for your god(s.) Christianity is about what God can do for you!

Yes, God demands that you approach Him His way, and He demands all of your praise, dedication and love. He is a jealous God. (Exodus 20:5) There are things God expects you to do, and not to do, as outlined in His Word. (Joshua 1:8)

But ultimately, Jesus Christ, more so than any other "deity," declares, "If you give Me all of you, I'll give you all of Me." Who gets the better end of this bargain? Without a doubt, we do.

We get salvation, forgiveness, acceptance, healing, love, joy, peace, protection, provision for our material needs, the list goes on and on. What does He get? Us. In all our imperfect, messed up ways. It boggles the mind.

So because of this, we state our belief that Jesus Christ is the "Way, the Truth and the Life," and no person can come to the Father but through their faith in Him. (John 14:6)

Salvation for a lost mankind is only through repentance of their sin. (1 John 1:9) To repent means to change one's mind: to acknowledge one has sinned, to define "sin" as what the Bible calls sin, and to turn away from it. It is only through the indwelling of the Holy Spirit that we are able to turn away from sin, leading a holy life dedicated solely unto the Lord God.

Salvation is a free gift that cannot be earned. There are no works, penance or rituals a person can do to be considered in right-standing with God. It is an act of graciousness on God's part to forgive your sins on the basis of Jesus' shed blood.

"For by grace you have been saved through faith, and that not of yourselves; it is the gift of God, not of works, lest anyone should boast." (Ephesians 2:8-9)

"But when the kindness and the love of God our Savior toward man appeared, not by works of righteousness which we have done, but according to His mercy He saved us, through the washing of regeneration and renewing of the Holy Spirit, whom He poured out on us abundantly through Jesus Christ our Savior, that having been justified by His grace we should become heirs according to the hope of eternal life." (Titus 3:4-7)

So what is our role in accepting this gift of salvation? Confession with our mouths, and belief in our hearts. It is not that difficult to become a born-again Christian.

"…That if you confess with your mouth the Lord Jesus and believe in your heart that God has raised Him from the dead, you will be saved. For with the heart one believes unto righteousness, and with the mouth confession is made unto salvation." (Romans 10:9-10)

ETERNITY

Excepting a few fringe sects, the vast majority of mainstream Christianity, Protestant and Catholic alike, believe in both Heaven and Hell as literal places, where the spirits of those who've died spend eternity.

For the born again, Spirit-filled Christian, we believe Hell to be a distinct, geographical place—it is not a state of mind, or simply being "apart from God."

There is no other state of "existence"—there is no Limbo, in the Catholic sense of the term, and there are no "lost souls" (ghosts.) There is also no state of Purgatory. Either Christ's atoning work on the cross was enough for all sins, or it wasn't. There is no "halfway" saved.

The Bible teaches that the dead are not "resting" in their graves, unconscious, until the Day of Judgment. When the spirit leaves the body at death, it either ascends to Heaven or descends to Hell.

"We are confident, I say, and willing rather to be absent from the body, and to be present with the Lord." (2 Corinthians 5:8)

Since Paul is stating that being "absent from the body" would mean he would be "present with the Lord," of necessity it means that when one dies, their spirit departs the body.

Jesus also taught that Hell is "outer darkness" (complete darkness); there will be "weeping and gnashing of teeth" (implying mental anguish and actual pain that can be felt); and He speaks of Hell being eternally on fire. (Matthew 8:12, 13:42, 18:9, 25:41)

In Mark 9:42-48, Jesus uses the phrase "Their worm does not die, and the fire is not quenched." There are several interpretations of what that undying "worm" is, ranging from simply poetic description—since the Greek word Gehenna spoke of a place outside the city where refuse and bodies were constantly burning, and maggots consumed the decaying matter—to literal demonic attack; that is, the demons themselves torture and torment the spirits in Hell.

Based on my personal experience, I believe I have a pretty good understanding of the "worm," and I share this in *Overwhelmed by the Spirit*. Also based on that experience, I am convinced the realm of Hell (Sheol, Hades, Gehenna) is in the belly of the earth; and I think it is comprised of more than one level, meaning there are levels of torment in Hell, depending on the actions of the person while on the earth before death.

If you're interested in my testimony, please read *Overwhelmed*, but because the Bible does not specifically teach that Hell is split into levels, I do not claim it is doctrine—rather, a personal belief.

According to Revelation 20:14-15, Hell (Hades) is a separate place than the Lake of Fire. Hell and the Lake of Fire were created for Satan and his demons; however, those whose names are not written in the Book of Life—those who have not accepted Jesus Christ as Lord and Savior prior to their death on earth—will be cast into the Lake, and this is called the "Second Death."

"But the cowardly, unbelieving, abominable, murderers, sexually immoral, sorcerers, idolaters, and all liars shall have their part in the lake which burns with fire and brimstone, which is the second death." (Revelation 21:8)

It is permanent and unchanging for all eternity. The Bible does not teach that there is an annihilation of souls—that after a specific time in torment, God just "blinks" those souls out of existence. Since we have been created in the image of God (Genesis 1:27), who is an eternal Spirit (Deuteronomy 33:27; John 4:24), our spirits are also, therefore, eternal.

The whole point of the Bible is to convince the reader there is a Hell, and how one can avoid going there after death. It is really that simple.

Conversely, those who make Christ their sole Savior, believing on Him to justify them when they die, ascend to Heaven, the realm of God the Father. There are a host of verses in the Bible describing Heaven, and I will list several here: Matthew 25:46; Luke 20:34-36, 23:43; John 5:29, 10:28, 14:2; Hebrews 11:16, 12:22-24, 13:14; 1 Peter 1:4; 2 Peter 3:13; Revelation 2:7, 4:1-11, 7:9, 21-22.

So what happens when you die? Your spirit will either go to Heaven or Hell, depending on whether or not you are born again.

Now, on to the resurrection of the dead. At the end of this Age (whenever that is: tomorrow, next decade, next century, no one but God knows; Matthew 24:36), the Lord Jesus Christ will appear in glory with the angels of Heaven, and those who have died in Christ will rise first. Then, those who are alive and born again at the moment of His appearance will be caught up into the air with Him. (1 Thessalonians 4:16-17) We will be changed into an incorruptible form (a glorified body like Jesus.) (1 Corinthians 15:51-52)

"For this corruptible must put on incorruption, and this mortal must put on immortality. So when this corruptible has put on incorruption, and this mortal has put on immortality, then shall be brought to pass the saying that is written: 'Death is swallowed up in victory. O Death, where is your sting? O Hades, where is your victory?' The sting of death is sin, and the strength of sin is the law. But thanks be to God, who gives us the victory through our Lord Jesus Christ." (1 Corinthians 15:53-57)

Now, there are varying viewpoints on whether this Second Coming of Christ is what is termed "the Rapture," that they are the same occurrence happening simultaneously, either before or after the Great Tribulation, when the wrath of God is poured out upon the unrighteous. (Matthew 24:21-29; Revelation 7:14) Or whether the Rapture, as we generally understand the term when we think of, say, the *Left Behind* series, is a separate event that occurs during some part of the Tribulation, at the beginning, middle, or end.

There are strong arguments for all theories, but since eschatology is conjecture, it's not in the scope of this book to defend or discount a particular theory. We cannot make a statement of faith on something not explicitly delineated in the Bible: *when* the Rapture occurs, only that it *does* occur.

Since everybody always asks me, if I had to label it, I would probably call myself a partial preterist and a partial historicist, but I am not entirely anti-futurist for all that, either, and I don't believe there is a need for division in the Body of Christ over eschatology, because the bottom line is, no one knows—we're probably all partially right and partially wrong. The future will take care of itself when it gets here.

There are levels of preterism, which basically means a person to varying degrees believes some (or all) biblical prophecy has *already* been fulfilled. So, for example, the Book of Daniel was fulfilled prior to the first century, and the Book of Revelation also describes poetically events that happened within the first century after Christ ascended (like, the destruction of Jerusalem in AD 70.)

Historicism believes biblical prophecy has been fulfilled in certain cases but has a continual fulfillment throughout the ages as well. So Daniel and Revelation can speak of AD 70 but could also have future application and fulfillment. There is a spirit of antichrist in the world today, there have been many antichrists throughout history (1 John 2:18, 4:3), and there may yet be "the Antichrist."

Futurism means eschatological prophecy has a future fulfillment—we will literally see a person who is the Antichrist sometime in the future. There will be a future, literal mark of the beast, so on and so forth.

I believe there are elements of all three. Some prophecy has been fulfilled, some has a future fulfillment, and some prophecy has multiple fulfillments throughout history. Some prophecy speaks of natural Israel, some speaks of spiritual Israel (that is us, the Body of Christ.) But we can apply principles in our lives from both.

Therefore, the entire Bible, from the Old Testament through John's Revelation, is applicable not only to the people at the time it was given, but has an application for us today, and will still be applicable to people in the future.

So yes, Jesus was speaking specifically to the church in Laodicea. (Revelation 3) But I believe there are "Laodicean" churches in existence today, and His admonition would apply to them just as it did to the literal Laodiceans.

This is why proper hermeneutics are so important when studying the Bible. The Old Testament must be interpreted in light of the New Testament. The Law must be interpreted through the light of Christ's fulfillment of that Law. The mercy of God must be studied alongside the wrath of God. I refer you to *Aletheia Eleutheroo*'s section on hermeneutical study for more information.

Now, personally I hope there *is* a secret rapture before the so-called Great Tribulation—sure would be nice to miss out on all that! But if not, the Lord's people will be protected no matter what. So my statement of faith is I most certainly believe in a catching away, I just don't know when that occurs.

Moving on, we also believe the unrighteous dead will be resurrected. The sea and Hell will give up their dead. (Revelation 20:13) And God will judge everyone according to their deeds. (Hebrews 4:13)

"For we must all appear before the judgment seat of Christ, that each one may receive the things done in the body, according to what he has done, whether good or bad. Knowing, therefore, the terror of the Lord, we persuade men; but we are well known to God, and I also trust are well known in your consciences." (2 Corinthians 5:10-11)

"Then I saw a great white throne and Him who sat on it, from whose face the earth and the heaven fled away. And there was found no place for them. And I saw the dead, small and great, standing before God, and books were opened. And another book was opened, which is the Book of Life. And the dead were judged according to their works, by the things which were written in the books. The sea gave up the dead who were in it, and Death and Hades delivered up the dead who were in them. And they were judged, each one according to his works. Then Death and Hades were cast into the lake of fire. This is the second death. And anyone not found written in the Book of Life was cast into the lake of fire." (Revelation 20:11-15)

Lastly, I believe in a literal Millennial Reign of Jesus Christ on this earth. (Revelation 20:1-10) That means that I believe the ultimate expression of Jesus' authority, and therefore the complete definition of "dominion living," only comes when Jesus sets His feet on the Mount of Olives and establishes a literal, earthly reign as King of all kings, Lord of all lords.

When it comes to millennial doctrine, I believe many tenants of amillennialism, postmillennialism and premillennialism are theologically incongruous with the Bible.

Some premillennialism doctrine is tied into ultrafuturist philosophy (putting dominion living "some time" in the future but never "today"), and taken to its extreme, it demeans our individual expression of power and authority through the present-day ministries of Jesus Christ and the Holy Spirit operating in our personal, day-to-day lives. This inaccurately displays the victorious living that Christians are supposed to be progressing into in their personal walks with the Lord.

Some postmillennialism doctrine is tied into an ultradominionism philosophy. In its extreme form, some believe that the sin principle itself (and therefore, sickness, disease, and even death) will be broken and removed *before* the Second Coming. That the earth's nations will already be transformed into utopian societies prior to Christ's return, and that when He does come a second time, we're simply turning an already perfected world over to Him. This extremity is also errant.

Amillennialism means that the vision John had in the Book of Revelation is just to be spiritually interpreted in our time frame of the moment we live in. Ergo, there would not be a literal thousand-year reign of Christ, and instead we are "reigning" with Him now in a spiritual sense. Part of this is true: we are to be ruling and reigning in our own lives in this day and age and within the spheres of influence that God gives to us.

I believe entire communities, perhaps even nations, will come to the saving knowledge of Jesus Christ prior to His return. But this spiritual kingdom residing within us will one day become a literal kingdom upon this earth. It is only then that we will see the complete manifestation of Christ's supreme authority on display before the whole world's population.

So to reiterate all this: I can accept some partial preterist and some partial futurist thought, but I'm really mostly an historicist; and I am a millennialist, as opposed to extreme a-, pre-, or postmillennial teachings.

I believe most teachings on eschatology have a past, present and future application, just as Old Testament prophecy can still be applied in the life of a Christian today. I'm not entirely "one way" or the "other," but I am firm in my stance that the Second Coming of Jesus institutes a true reign of Christ upon the earth. The spiritual Kingdom that resides in each believer today will have a future, natural expression as well.

"Then I saw an angel coming down from heaven, having the key to the bottomless pit and a great chain in his hand. He laid hold of the dragon, that serpent of old, who is the Devil and Satan, and bound him for a thousand years; and he cast him into the bottomless pit, and shut him up, and set a seal on him, so that he should deceive the nations no more till the thousand years were finished. But after these things he must be released for a little while." (Revelation 20:1-3)

"The wolf also shall dwell with the lamb, the leopard shall lie down with the young goat, the calf and the young lion and the fatling together; and a little child shall lead them. The cow and the bear shall graze; their young ones shall lie down together; and the lion shall eat straw like the ox. The nursing child shall play by the cobra's hole, and the weaned child shall put his hand in the viper's den." (Isaiah 11:6-8)

To sum up this statement of faith, I believe the righteous who are born again are rewarded with eternal life forever in Heaven. I also believe the unrighteous receive everlasting punishment in Hell.

There are a couple comments I'd like to make that I think fit well in this chapter on eternity, based on some things I've heard being taught in Charismatic circles lately. I do not believe that time is relative, in the sense that we can travel backward or forward in time, whether physically, mentally, or spiritually. I believe this is vain imagination, which the Bible tells us to cast down. (Romans 1:21; 2 Corinthians 10:5-7) We cannot go into the future, and we cannot change the past. We live solely in the present.

Secondly, I disagree with the concepts of theophostic counseling. Basically, the implication of theophostics is one has to apply the principles of metaphysical science to, say, a particular lie or misconception a person has about whatever bondage one may be facing. Only after that can the truth of God's Word be applied correctly to break off that bondage.

I believe it is the truth of God's Word alone, applied in faith directly to the area of need, that sets a person free. It takes nothing more and nothing less. Nothing needs to be added to God's Word to make it effective, if you mix what you hear with faith.

"So then faith comes by hearing, and hearing by the word of God." (Romans 10:17)

"For indeed the gospel was preached to us as well as to them; but the word which they heard did not profit them, not being mixed with faith in those who heard it." (Hebrews 4:2)

"And you shall know the truth, and the truth shall make you free." (John 8:32)

"Sanctify them by Your truth. Your word is truth." (John 17:17)

Further, I do not believe we have to "convince" God to move on our behalves, in the sense of us pleading our case before a heavenly tribunal. In my studies, I have found these concepts extra-scriptural, and in some cases, out-and-out heretical. Again, we must stay rooted in the simplicity of the centrality of the cross.

Everything that God will ever do for us, has already been done—we need nothing more from Him, and all of His gifts toward us are already "yes and amen" through Jesus Christ. (2 Corinthians 1:20) We don't have to convince Him to "do" anything, only believe and appropriate through faith the provisions that the cross has already provided. (John 11:40)

This applies to financial needs (Philippians 4:19), physical healing (1 Peter 2:24), mental health (2 Timothy 1:17), emotional wellness (Psalm 147:3; 1 Peter 5:7), deliverance from demonic oppression (Matthew 8:16), and wisdom on a decision we need to make. (James 1:5) We do not have to ascertain God's will concerning any "need" we present Him.

I think Paul's admonition to Timothy is applicable in just about every "new" thing we hear concerning how God operates now:

"For the time will come when they will not endure sound doctrine, but according to their own desires, because they have itching ears, they will heap up for themselves teachers; and they will turn their ears away from the truth, and be turned aside to fables." (2 Timothy 4:3-4)

When Jesus said, "It is finished" (John 19:30), He meant it.

The Church

What do we mean when we say, "the Church"? In essence, the Church, or the "Body of Christ," is simply the unity and spiritual connection of all true believers in the Lord Jesus Christ. If you are born again, no matter what denomination or church (little "c") you belong to, you are a part of the Body of Christ. We are all in the same singular, universal Church as believing Christians.

The born again Catholic (yes, there are many!) attending mass in Boston is my brother or sister in the Lord as much as the fundamentalist East Texas Baptist, or the Spirit-filled, tongue-talking Californian prophet sitting in the chair next to me on Sunday morning. Age, race, gender, geographical location, skin color, hair color, eye color, political affiliation—so long as we're all professing salvation through Jesus Christ alone, we're a part of His Church.

I've met Amish and Mennonite folks who were truly born again. It boggles my mind that they would remain under such a form of legalism, but I certainly am in no position to say, "They cannot be saved." That's a dangerous stance to take.

So the questions I get: "Can a member of the *insert just about any traditional, religious sect of Christianity here* church be saved?", the answer is well, yes. Although I don't know why they'd continue in that traditional religious setting after a genuine salvation experience, there are some who do. Usually, in time, the Holy Spirit will lead them into a greater understanding, just as with any sect of Christianity, Protestant or Catholic, and they may decide to leave that church affiliation at some point. If you're truly seeking, you will find. I've been saved half a century and I don't claim to be perfected yet.

I don't care so much what you call yourself: do you believe Jesus Christ is the only way to get to Heaven? Is He your singular Lord and Savior? Have you confessed and repented of your sins, are you walking a Christian lifestyle as outlined in the Bible? Then you're born again, and you are a part of His Body. The rest will work itself out as long as you're yielding to Him. I think that's what Paul was talking about in Philippians 2 and 1 Corinthians 1. Jesus warned against sectarianism in Mark 9, knowing it would lead to much of the garbage we as Christians face today within our own groups. Most of His issues weren't with the tax collectors and sinners so much as with the "righteous" Pharisees and Sadducees.

Again, that's not to say there isn't a "right" and a "wrong" here—I am firmly against Universalism/inclusivism (remember, that means "all faiths lead to God," no matter what you call Him) in all its facets. Jesus is not New Age. You can't continue practicing neo-pagan witchcraft and say, "But I've accepted Jesus as my Lord and Savior." If you had, you wouldn't still be practicing witchcraft! That's like a Louisianan voodoo priest saying he "loves Jesus very much." Is he born again? I have no problem saying, "No, he's not."

But the fact still remains, if you are *truly* born again, no matter your denomination or local church affiliation, you are a member of His Church.

"For as the body is one and has many members, but all the members of that one body, being many, are one body, so also is Christ. For by one Spirit we were all baptized into one body—whether Jews or Greeks, whether slaves or free… Now you are the body of Christ, and members individually." (1 Corinthians 12:12-13, 27)

"And He put all things under His feet, and gave Him to be head over all things to the church, which is His body, the fullness of Him who fills all in all." (Ephesians 1:22-23)

So, what is the purpose of this Church? Above all else— above all the wonderful community programs, feeding and clothing the poor, housing orphans, hospital visits, marital counseling, addiction rehabilitation, dynamic praise and worship, societal change, etc., etc.—the primary function of the Church is the ministry of evangelism.

I think most concepts of dominion living are fantastic: changing the surrounding community where the local church is set through its various outreaches and programs, wielding political influence to affect a change in local society—all of this is important, don't get me wrong. But the thrust of every local church should be to bring in the lost, first and foremost.

"Then Jesus went about all the cities and villages, teaching in their synagogues, preaching the gospel of the kingdom, and healing every sickness and every disease among the people. But when He saw the multitudes, He was moved with compassion for them, because they were weary and scattered, like sheep having no shepherd. Then He said to His disciples, 'The harvest truly is plentiful, but the laborers are few. Therefore pray the Lord of the harvest to send out laborers into His harvest.'" (Matthew 9:35-38)

Evangelism is proclaiming the truth of the Gospel, the plan of salvation, at every opportunity we have. I take evangelism a step further than traditional denominations and say the Gospel must be preached with the accompanying signs and wonders that back up the validity of that salvation message. (Mark 16:20; Romans 15:19)

Ergo, "There is only one Way to Heaven, that is through belief in the Lord Jesus Christ. To prove He is the right Way, and all the other ways are false, bring up your sick, and Jesus will heal them."

Is that bold? Yes. Does it work? Yes. I find it a much more effective form of evangelism than simply bringing the homeless into a soup kitchen and saying, "Jesus loves you." Again, I'm not knocking that form of evangelism—I'm saying, do the soup kitchen *and* lay hands on the sick. Preach the *whole* Gospel of Christ.

I think this is in a similar vein as Jesus' rebuke against the religious leaders of His day in Matthew 23. Oftentimes we neglect the "weightier matters" of a true representation of Jesus Christ, and so it only presents *half* of what Jesus is all about.

Don't misunderstand my intent: good deeds matter surely. "Therefore, as we have opportunity, let us do good to all, especially to those who are of the household of faith." (Galatians 6:10) And even to people who don't like us, Romans 12:20-21 tells us, "Therefore 'if your enemy is hungry, feed him; if he is thirsty, give him a drink; for in so doing you will heap coals of fire on his head.' Do not be overcome by evil, but overcome evil with good." But Jesus is more than just food or drink or good deeds.

Of course Jesus doesn't want the homeless to starve, but what does it profit a man to gain the whole world and lose his own soul? (Mark 8:36) He wants us to give them the bread and *the* Bread.

The purpose of the Body of Christ is to represent our Head accurately to the people at large in the name of evangelism. Every believer has a responsibility to present their Lord and Savior correctly and fully at every opportunity they are given. It's not just for pastors and church leaders—we are all supposed to be "evangelists." The entire Body in operation.

"And Jesus came and spoke to them, saying, 'All authority has been given to Me in heaven and on earth. Go therefore and make disciples of all the nations, baptizing them in the name of the Father and of the Son and of the Holy Spirit, teaching them to observe all things that I have commanded you; and lo, I am with you always, even to the end of the age.' Amen." (Matthew 28:18-20)

"For the Scripture says, 'Whoever believes on Him will not be put to shame.' For there is no distinction between Jew and Greek, for the same Lord over all is rich to all who call upon Him. For 'whoever calls on the name of the Lord shall be saved.' How then shall they call on Him in whom they have not believed? And how shall they believe in Him of whom they have not heard? And how shall they hear without a preacher? And how shall they preach unless they are sent? As it is written: 'How beautiful are the feet of those who preach the gospel of peace, who bring glad tidings of good things!'" (Romans 10:11-15)

The second purpose of the Church, after evangelizing and bringing people into the Body, is to disciple those people and help them grow in their relationship with Christ. Let's take our previous examples of a person in a traditional religious group who has had a salvation experience. Is he or she born again? Yes, but they are an "infant" in the Body of Christ and staying in their home religion may keep them an infant their entire lives. This is sad.

Or let's say there's a born-again Baptist who loves the Lord with all his or her heart. Their home religion may keep them from entering into the fullness God has to offer in the name of baptism in the Holy Spirit. This is also sad.

Then let's take the person who's irreligious: the Church's primary "target audience," as it were. The former atheist, or the once-churchgoer who's slipped away over the years. Once that person comes, or comes back, into the Body of Christ, they too need to be trained and equipped, otherwise there is a risk of their falling into legalism and religiosity, or into extrascriptural beliefs, fanaticism, or back into sinful carnality and sensuality (looseness of moral living), thwarting their full expression as a member of that Body. This is perhaps the saddest.

When I hear of the indictments brought against religion from those on the outside, I often find myself thinking, "I know what you mean." I do not like religion. Religion—as opposed to a true, vibrant relationship with Jesus Christ and fellowship with His true, sincere Body—can be more damaging in thwarting the full potential of people than most things the world can throw at them.

That's why God always starts with the Church before dealing with the world. To whom much is given, much is required. (Luke 12:48) Or we could go all web-slinging superhero and say, "With great power comes great responsibility."

The true Church is not meant to be some "ol' boys' clique," but rather, it's supposed to be a training ground, an equipping center, to lead that newly born-again person into a deeper understanding and relationship with his or her Savior. The true Church wants to present the full Gospel to the people, so that they can reach their full potential in

Christ. The true Church wants to show the irreligious that true religion is taking care of your fellow man's needs and keeping yourself untainted from the garbage that is in the world. (James 1:27)

As that true "religion" develops, the Lord will make sure they begin to recognize where their particular sect of Christianity has it right and has it wrong. And yes, my dear reader, all sects of Christianity have *something* right and *something* wrong about them. The reason the Body is not yet perfected is because it is comprised of *people*. But don't worry, Jesus knew what He was doing when He set it up this way.

This is why relationship is so important. I need you, you need me, we all need the Word. It takes the entire Body, iron sharpening iron (Proverbs 27:17), for us to grow into our full potentials as members of that Body.

The Church is not a set of rules and rituals to make God (or other people) like you. As Jesus told the scribe in Mark 12: "The first of all the commandments is: 'Hear, O Israel, the Lord our God, the Lord is one. And you shall love the Lord your God with all your heart, with all your soul, with all your mind, and with all your strength.' This is the first commandment. And the second, like it, is this: 'You shall love your neighbor as yourself.' There is no other commandment greater than these." (Verses 29-31)

The true "religion" of the Church, in fact everything the Bible has to say, hangs on these two commandments. (Matthew 22:40; James 1:27) And for those of us who "get it" throughout the course of our lives, to them Jesus says, "You are not far from the kingdom of God." (Mark 12:34)

HUMAN LIVING

This last section is a quick statement of faith on the institution of the family. It seemed appropriate to outline what mainstream Christianity believes is God's plan concerning marriage and the family, since it is one of those "old fashioned" definitions that has come under so much scrutiny since the turn of the century.

Of all the commandments in the Bible, the ones given on human sexuality are among the most important to one's Christian walk. It's a big deal to God, and therefore, should be a big deal to us.

Paul wrote to the Thessalonians: "For ye know what commandments we gave you by the Lord Jesus. For this is the will of God, even your sanctification, that ye should abstain from fornication: that every one of you should know how to possess his vessel in sanctification and honour; not in the lust of concupiscence, even as the Gentiles which know not God: that no man go beyond and defraud his brother in any matter: because that the Lord is the avenger of all such, as we also have forewarned you and testified. For God hath not called us unto uncleanness, but unto holiness. He therefore that despiseth, despiseth not man, but God, who hath also given unto us his holy Spirit." (1 Thessalonians 4:2-8 KJV)

I use the KJV, because I think it renders Paul's admonishment perfectly clear. I paraphrase here, but it's almost as if Paul is saying, "Look, if you can't do anything else 'right,' at least get this right: stay away from immorality." Why is this such a big deal? Is it because God enjoys shackling the human race with an archaic, Puritanical system of rules? Certainly not.

Paul, again, gives the reason: "Flee sexual immorality. Every sin that a man does is outside the body, but he who commits sexual immorality sins against his own body." (1 Corinthians 6:18)

The apostle makes it as clear as he can: "Do you not know that the unrighteous will not inherit the kingdom of God? Do not be deceived. Neither fornicators, nor idolaters, nor adulterers, nor homosexuals, nor sodomites, nor thieves, nor covetous, nor drunkards, nor revilers, nor extortioners will inherit the kingdom of God." (1 Corinthians 6:9-10)

(As an aside, and not to be too graphic, but in an effort to cover the entire gamut of immorality, so there is no confusion, Paul delineates between "homosexuals"—those who submit to homosexuality; that is, catamites—and "sodomites"— male homosexuals. However, lesbianism, bisexuality and omnisexuality are all under the umbrella of homosexuality.)

"For this reason God gave them up to vile passions. For even their women exchanged the natural use for what is against nature. Likewise also the men, leaving the natural use of the woman, burned in their lust for one another, men with men committing what is shameful, and receiving in themselves the penalty of their error which was due." (Romans 1:26-27)

I am not sure how more clearly the Bible can make God's stance on "alternative lifestyles." Words like vile, unnatural, shameful, error. This modern concept that "God made me this way" is as entirely unscriptural as "living together before marriage."

I have been asked numerous times by members of the LGBTQ community how I get around that most of them believe they were born with their sexuality. I answer that yes, I believe one can be born with such proclivities, as much as one can be born with, say, an addictive personality. This is why the tenet of original sin discussed earlier is so important. The Bible calls this *iniquity*: being "bent" toward sin, an inherited leaning against God's decrees. Just because someone is born with a particular leaning, it is still an active choice to engage in activity the Bible calls "sinful."

Okay, so to state it clearly: true Christians believe God created man and woman to complement and complete each other. (Genesis 2:24) The marriage union is supposed to reflect the union of God to mankind. (Ephesians 5:22-33) There are many instances where God defines the worship of any other being or thing as prostitution and adultery. (Jeremiah 13:27; Hosea 4:12 as two examples.) That's how strong a sentiment He has toward His relationship with you.

"And He answered and said to them, 'Have you not read that He who made them at the beginning "made them male and female," and said, "For this reason a man shall leave his father and mother and be joined to his wife, and the two shall become one flesh"? So then, they are no longer two but one flesh. Therefore what God has joined together, let not man separate.'" (Matthew 19:4-6)

God built the fundamental organization of human society on the foundation of marriage. We've all heard the adage, "It all starts in the home." This structure, instituted by God, begins and ends with humanity, and we should not extrapolate an "alternative definition" using nature as the basis, since we are the only beings in nature "made in His image." (Genesis 1:27)

Now, while I am aware that polygamy and homosexuality exist in the animal kingdom, and many members of the LGBTQ community utilize this as a proof that gay activity is "hardwired" into the genetic code—though it boggles my mind, since at some point, it seems all animals recognize the need for heterosexuality in order to propagate their species—the existence of polygamy and homosexuality in the animal kingdom should not be used to define ethical human living, any more than saying, "Well, lions eat zebras alive, why shouldn't we?" Monkeys will also play with their excrement, and dogs return to their own vomit. (Proverbs 26:11) Should we? I believe that's a weak argument using reverse logic. The animal kingdom reflects the depravity of the unregenerate human condition, not the other way around. (Romans 8:19-23)

Okay, so moving on from that unsavory aside, true Christians espouse that marriage is supposed to be a monogamous union of one man and one woman, and sexual activity should only be expressed in the context of that marriage. In today's society, we now have to define "man" and "woman" as the biological, genetic gender one has at the moment of birth.

Yes, I recognize that there are instances of genetic malformation in the womb, and in some cases, the gender must be decided; but these are rarer occurrences, and, again, should not be used as a guideline to identify all of society's definitions for gender or human sexuality, any more than the horrific acts of rape and incest, or the sad fact that birth can sometimes put the mother's life at risk, should be used to justify abortion, across the board, in matters of convenience.

Along this line of thinking, true Christians believe that all human life is sacred from the moment of conception all the way to its natural end.

This means while I believe modern medicine can assist a person in passing away with as little pain and as much dignity as possible—pain management drugs and medically induced coma, etc.—and we most certainly can "let nature take its course" (that is, "do not resuscitate" clauses in living wills and the like), I do not believe out-and-out assisted suicide is morally or ethically "righteous."

According to the Bible we have an obligation to show concern for the needs, emotional, physical, and spiritual, of each human being, helping whenever and wherever we can by any ethical means. Every human life has intrinsic value and worth, because it is a representation of the creation of God made in His image.

"For You formed my inward parts; You covered me in my mother's womb." (Psalm 139:13) The word "covered" is better translated "wove."

If life does not begin at the moment of conception, then Jesus was simply a fetus in Mary's womb, nothing more than tissue. However, when He prophesied of Himself in the Book of Isaiah, He declared: "Listen, O coastlands, to Me, and take heed, you peoples from afar! The LORD has called Me from the womb; from the matrix of My mother He has made mention of My name." (Isaiah 49:1)

God said of Jeremiah: "Before I formed you in the womb I knew you; before you were born I sanctified you; I ordained you a prophet to the nations." (Jeremiah 1:5)

Now, on the other side of the coin, since life begins at the moment of conception, this means I completely reject the notion of preexistent souls in Heaven, waiting earthly bodies to inhabit. This teaching is not supported in Scripture, and any doctrine you read or hear that is tied into this notion is errant from the outset. There is no "Chamber of Souls" in Heaven, any more than there is a "Limbo of Infants."

Romans 9:11-14 and verses like Jeremiah 1:5 speak to God's foreknowledge and omniscience, not premortal existence. And while I am not firm in my stance with those who believe in traducianism (that the spirit is created through natural generation by the uniting of sperm and egg, just as the physical body is created) or those who believe in creationism (that the spirit is created by God Himself at the moment of conception and "poured" into the zygote), I am as firm against preexistence as I am against reincarnation.

Summary Statement

In summation, I believe the bedrock of the Christian faith is the Bible, inerrant, infallible and inspired, which expressly outlines who God is (and is not) and delivers His commandments to a fallen mankind, which, to a person, has rebelled against God and is born in a state of spiritual death and sin, wholly incapable of redeeming itself.

Apart from God's intervention, through the sacrifice of His Son, Jesus Christ, who is very God Himself, while also completely Man, humanity would by no means be able to keep those commandments in the Bible without the indwelling of His Spirit in a born-again experience, which is a free gift offered to all mankind through faith in the justifying work of the blood of Jesus alone, apart from any works or religious ritual. There is no other means by which mankind may approach God—all other religions and all other gods are false.

Subsequent to the new birth, I believe in the infilling of the Holy Spirit, with the evidence of speaking in tongues, which enables the believer to live a holy, righteous lifestyle that is pleasing to God, providing the person with boldness to share their faith and an anointing of power, through the delegated supreme authority of the Lord Jesus Christ, to see signs, wonders, miracles, healing for the mind, soul and body, and provision for all material needs—all the acts of Jesus while He was on the earth—duplicated in one's day-to-day life.

I believe the primary purpose of this infilling is given in order to meet the needs of my fellow man, sharing with them the full Gospel of the Kingdom of God, so that any and all may come to the saving knowledge of Jesus Christ. Without that saving grace, all mankind is doomed to eternal, literal punishment, and we as believing Christians are in a race to present the plan of salvation to everyone we can, before it is too late.

This is my statement of faith. Amen.

Dr. James E. Maloney
Argyle, Texas
1 January 2019

PRAYER FOR SALVATION

Dear Father in heaven, I believe that You sent Your Son, Jesus Christ, to die on the cross for the sins of the whole world. I believe in the total sacrifice of Christ, and that only His blood can wash away sin. I now ask for forgiveness of my sins through the blood of Jesus. I give my life to You, Lord Jesus, and ask You to come into my heart. Make me a brand-new creature by Your Spirit, that I may be born again. I turn away from the world and sin, and by Your help, will become more like You each day. I receive Your free gift of salvation now, realizing I am saved by faith in Your grace. I take You for my own personal Savior, Jesus, and believe that as I repent, You are now making me Your child. I praise and thank You for salvation."

> *Friend, if you meant this prayer, God will begin a wonderful work in your life today. Your relationship with Him will grow as you study His Word (the Bible), talk with Him in prayer and attend a Spirit-filled church. Isolation is a tool of the enemy, so get involved in a Bible-preaching church and fellowship with other Christians.*

PRAYER FOR BAPTISM IN THE SPIRIT

Dear Lord Jesus, I believe in my heart that I am born again, and I confess with my mouth that you are my Savior and my Lord. I ask for the free gift of baptism in the Holy Spirit, with the evidence of speaking in tongues, believing I receive Him now as I pray in faith. I know it is Your desire that Your Spirit would fill me completely, pouring out as a River of living water that will never run dry. As I yield my life to You day-by-day, I believe Your Spirit will empower me to live in holiness and boldness, and I want to yield my voice to Him to pray through me with a heavenly prayer language. I thank You, Lord, for the gift of the Holy Spirit, and I welcome Him now."

> *Friend, after you have prayed this prayer, receive the Holy Spirit and begin to use your heavenly language. It is an act of faith, and the Spirit will meet your faith. He does not "take over" your lips, voice and tongue. At first, it may be one or two words with a stammering lip, like a baby talks, but by reason of use, it will develop into a full language.*

Prayer for Healing

Dear Jesus, I believe I have a covenant right as Your child, one bought by Your blood, to be free from sickness and disease, mentally, emotionally and physically. Your sacrifice at Calvary was equally for my physical health as for my spiritual salvation. It is the same blood doing the same work, throughout eternity. I call upon Your name, Your authority, over every manner of sickness and disease, and I claim divine healing and health as my right, justified as I am through my faith in You. I believe I have received healing in faith, and I expect my body to line up with the Word, which declares by Your stripes I *was* healed. Thank You, Lord!"

Friend, physical healing is an act of faith. Begin to do those things you were previously unable to do. Often, there is a time of improvement before a full manifestation of healing—do not cast away your confidence, which has great recompense of reward. It is not a lack of faith to continue taking prescribed medication or treatment until your physician tells you otherwise. Be wise in your faith.

The Apostles' Creed

I believe in God, the Father almighty, Creator of heaven and earth. I believe in Jesus Christ, God's only Son, our Lord, who was conceived by the Holy Spirit, born of the Virgin Mary, suffered under Pontius Pilate, was crucified, died, and was buried; He descended to the dead. On the third day He rose again; He ascended into heaven, He is seated at the right hand of the Father, and He will come to judge the living and the dead. I believe in the Holy Spirit, the holy catholic Church, the communion of saints, the forgiveness of sins, the resurrection of the body, and the life everlasting. Amen.

Author's note: The word "catholic" has intentionally been left uncapitalized, referring to the universal, ecumenical Church (the body of Christ) as opposed to a particular sect or denomination.

The Nicene Creed

We believe in one God, the Father, the Almighty maker of heaven and earth, of all that is, seen and unseen.

We believe in one Lord, Jesus Christ, the only Son of God, eternally begotten of the Father, God from God, Light from Light, true God from true God, begotten, not made, of one Being with the Father. Through Him all things were made.

For us men and for our salvation He came down from heaven: by the power of the Holy Spirit He became incarnate from the Virgin Mary, and was made man. For our sake He was crucified under Pontius Pilate; He suffered death and was buried. On the third day He rose again in accordance with the Scriptures; He ascended into heaven and is seated at the right hand of the Father. He will come again in glory to judge the living and the dead, and His kingdom will have no end.

We believe in the Holy Spirit, the Lord, the Giver of Life, who proceeds from the Father and the Son. With the Father and the Son He is worshipped and glorified. He has spoken through the Prophets.

We believe in one holy catholic and apostolic Church. We acknowledge one baptism for the forgiveness of sins. We look for the resurrection of the dead, and the life of the world to come. Amen.

About the Author

James Maloney has been in full-time ministry for over forty years as president of Dove on the Rise International. As a well-respected prophetic voice, James' ministry expression is marked by a powerful sign-and-wonder flow, heavily geared toward healing for the mind, soul and body.

But James' life began with abuse, rejection and fear. As a teenager, facing suicidal thoughts, he cried out for an answer: "God, if You're really real, You're going to have to reveal Yourself to me, because I can't take this anymore!"

Jesus Christ provided that answer, appearing in a cloud of glory with two outstretched hands: "I have heard your cry for acceptance. I have heard your cry for reality, and I love you just the way that you are."

Since that life-altering encounter, the Lord's anointing and grace have manifested through James' ministry in a prophetic seer operation, where specific details about people's conditions are supernaturally revealed, thereby creating faith in Jesus Christ to receive their miracle. To God's honor alone, this panoramic flow has been consistently used to dissolve metal in people's bodies, to create or recreate limbs, to liquefy tumors and pacemakers, to open blind eyes and deaf ears, and much more!

As an accomplished theologian, James holds a D.D., a Th.D. and a Ph.D. He taught in Bible schools for over twenty years and has authored several exciting books: *The Dancing Hand of God, The Panoramic Seer, Overwhelmed by the Spirit, Aletheia Eleutheroo, The Lord in the Fires, Living above the Snake Line,* and *The Wounded Cry.* He is also the compiler of the best-selling *Ladies of Gold,* the collected teachings of Frances Metcalfe and the Golden Candlestick.

James and his wife, Joy, live in the Dallas-Fort Worth area with their grown children and grandchildren.

For more information, please contact:
Dove on the Rise International
P.O. Box 1166
Argyle, Texas 76226-1166
www.doveontherise.com

Printed in the United States
By Bookmasters